Select Titles in Contemporary Issues in the Middle East

Being There, Being Here: Palestinian Writings in the World
Maurice Ebileeni

Generations of Dissent: Intellectuals, Cultural Production,
and the State in the Middle East and North Africa
Alexa Firat and R. Shareah Taleghani, eds.

The Lost Orchard: The Palestinian-Arab Citrus Industry, 1850–1950
Mustafa Kabha and Nahum Karlinsky

Ottoman Children and Youth during World War I
Nazan Maksudyan

Readings in Syrian Prison Literature: The Poetics of Human Rights
R. Shareah Taleghani

Turkey's State Crisis: Institutions, Reform, and Conflict
Bülent Aras

Understanding Hezbollah: The Hegemony of Resistance
Abed T. Kanaaneh

Victims of Commemoration: The Architecture and Violence
of Confronting the Past in Turkey
Eray Çaylı

For a full list of titles in this series, visit
https://press.syr.edu/supressbook-series
/contemporary-issues-in-the-middle-east/.

LIFE ON DRUGS IN IRAN

Contemporary Issues in the Middle East
Mehran Kamrava, *Series Editor*

LIFE on DRUGS in IRAN

BETWEEN PRISON AND REHAB

Nahid Rahimipour Anaraki

Syracuse University Press

Copyright © 2022 by Syracuse University Press
Syracuse, New York 13244-5290

All Rights Reserved

First Edition 2022

22 23 24 25 26 27   6 5 4 3 2 1

∞ The paper used in this publication meets the minimum requirements
of the American National Standard for Information Sciences—Permanence
of Paper for Printed Library Materials, ANSI Z39.48-1992.

For a listing of books published and distributed by Syracuse University Press,
visit https://press.syr.edu.

ISBN: 978-0-8156-3773-8 (hardcover)
978-0-8156-3783-7 (paperback)
978-0-8156-5567-1 (e-book)

Library of Congress Cataloging-in-Publication Data

Names: Anaraki, Nahid Rahimipour, author.
Title: Life on drugs in Iran : between prison and rehab / Nahid Rahimipour Anaraki.
Description: First Edition. | Syracuse, New York : Syracuse University Press, 2022. |
    Series: Contemporary issues in the Middle East | Includes bibliographical
    references and index.
Identifiers: LCCN 2022015873 (print) | LCCN 2022015874 (ebook) |
    ISBN 9780815637738 (hardcover) | ISBN 9780815637837 (paperback) |
    ISBN 9780815655671 (ebook)
Subjects: LCSH: Prisoners—Drug use—Iran. | Drug addicts—Rehabilitation—Iran. |
    Prisons—Iran. | Correctional institutions—Iran.
Classification: LCC HV8836.5 .A49 2022 (print) | LCC HV8836.5 (ebook) |
    DDC 365/.660955—dc23/eng/20220604
LC record available at https://lccn.loc.gov/2022015873
LC ebook record available at https://lccn.loc.gov/2022015874

Manufactured in the United States of America

Contents

Acknowledgments   *vii*

Introduction   *1*

1. History: *A Journey from Opium to Heroin and Methadone*   *17*

2. Accursed Pathway   *32*

3. Prison: *The Dehumanization Ceremony*   *39*

4. NA: *Stretching Normality*   *74*

5. Contested Identity in Prison and Rehabilitation   *111*

Conclusion   *123*

References   *131*

Index   *151*

Acknowledgments

I would Like to express my gratitude and appreciation to all those whose assistance made this book possible. My sincere gratitude to Dr. Anton Oleinik, who patiently listened and guided me in articulating the central thesis of this book. Dr. Oleinik was supportive throughout the process of bringing this book to fruition, and his constructive feedback on an early draft of the manuscript rendered greater clarity, consistency, and organization to the book. I am also particularly grateful to Mr. Meghraj Mukhopadhyay for editing and polishing the final version of the manuscript. Also, I would like to thank my participants whose invaluable and rich experiences inspired, accompanied, and guided me throughout this journey. Finally, as with all my projects, this book would not have been feasible without the full support of my family members—Shadi, Javad, Shohre, Sadiye, Farshid, and Kian. I would like to especially thank my father, Ali; without his financial assistance, this project would not have been accomplished.

The cover picture is a Narcotic Anonymous (NA) meeting in Iran, taken by one of the attending NA members. The setting is familiar to some members who have been gathering there from 8:00 to 9:00 p.m. every night for a decade.

Previously published material about prison subculture is from *Prison in Iran: A Known Unknown* (Anaraki 2021) reproduced in modified form with permission from the publisher, Palgrave Macmillan.

LIFE ON DRUGS IN IRAN

Introduction

Medicalization

To begin my research regarding the lived experiences of people who use substances[1] in governmental and nongovernmental organization (NGO) institutions, I traveled to Iran to conduct in-depth interviews. Before my journey from Canada to the Islamic Republic of Iran (Iran), I received several comments questioning the feasibility of the research that I planned to conduct. This was of no concern to me, as I was mistakenly comparing the planned research with a 2012 study I had conducted regarding incarcerated women and children. At that time, I had been granted permission to access a women's ward (*band-e nesvan*) with the assistance of an NGO. However, challenges with gaining access to the field of study arose early in the summer of 2017. Several people had intervened to help me access drug treatment, recovery, and harm reduction centers, including lawyers and NGO managers. Some of the mediators were predominantly individuals who were using or had used substances, including Narcotics Anonymous (NA) members. Few permissions were granted, and the relevant decisions were relayed verbally over the phone to me before I learned of the organization's location; some were illegal treatment centers that would only disclose their location after checking with my sponsors.[2] In some cases, such as state-run organizations, the exact location was not disclosed until the very last moment, once the gatekeepers[3] could verify additional

---

1. Alternative to stigmatizing terms such as drug users or drug abusers.
2. In field work, sponsors are those who introduce the researcher to the field.
3. Gatekeepers give formal permission for field research.

2   Life on Drugs in Iran

information and accompany me to the organization. I was given permission to return to the center occasionally to conduct interviews immediately after the first meeting with the managers where the gatekeepers were present.

After several challenging weeks, one of the most popular state-run male treatment camps in a poor and high-crime neighborhood agreed to grant me access. I had not been provided with the exact location since I arranged the appointment with a gatekeeper who had recovered at the same camp. I picked him up, as he lived in the low-income neighborhood nearby. Before reaching the center, he indirectly suggested that we buy fruits and sweets for its clients: "It's much better to not go there *dast-e khali* (empty-handed). They don't always have dessert or fruits." With a large plate of sweets and a wooden box of fruits, we entered the treatment center. The door was open, and one client was sprinkling water and sweeping the road. A law enforcement officer was sitting inside the camp by the front door, closely watching traffic. While I was discussing my research objectives with the manager, one patient offered me some tea. He had recovered three years ago under the supervision of the manager and was recruited by the center while he was an NA member. The manager was in long-term recovery and also an active NA member. He said:

> Did you see this poor man? The day that his family forcefully brought him here, they begged to keep him here by all means. They apparently tried all the camps but had no success. Of course, he tried to escape several times, but we kept him here by force, you know. They go crazy, especially during the first weeks. We do everything to keep them: cold showers, yelling, beating, whatever. Now he is clean and regularly attends the NA meetings.

When I interviewed the patient who offered me tea, everyone, including the manager, moved next door to smoke hookah and drink *chayi nabat* (tea with rock candy).

This was not my first encounter with so-called "medicalization" as a niche or recess of "criminalization." The constant surveillance of law enforcement officers at the front door and use of coercive methods under the slogan of a treatment-oriented approach reminded me of the coexistence of methadone maintenance treatment (MMT) and drugs in prison. Inspired by the notion of medicalization, my aim was to articulate the lived experiences of people who use substances by focusing on the impact of criminalization and medicalization usually presented under the disguise of scientific treatment. Although Michel Foucault did not necessarily use the concept of "medicalization," he did address the roots of objectification of man (i.e., denote a person as a "case" rather than a "human being") through the emergence of new medical discourse. In *The Birth of the Clinic* (1973), he described the "medical gaze" as the new "way of seeing" patients, whereby the doctor's question "what is the matter with you?" is replaced by "where does it hurt?" (Foucault 1973, xviii).

In other words, for the first time, man became the object of the science. As Foucault states, this was the moment "human sciences" and "technologies of power" emerged—the interrelation called "power/knowledge."

> First the hospital, then the school, then, later, the workshop were not simply "reordered" by the disciplines; they became, thanks to them, apparatuses such that any mechanism of objectification could be used in them as an instrument of subjection, and any growth of power could give rise in them to possible branches of knowledge; it was this link, proper to the technological systems, that made possible within the disciplinary element the formation of clinical medicine, psychiatry, child psychology, educational psychology and the rationalization of labour. It is a double process, then: an epistemological "thaw" through a refinement of power relations; a multiplication of the effects of power through the formation and accumulation of new forms of knowledge. (Foucault 1979, 224)

Specifically, Foucault argued that nineteenth-century medicine was applied according to "the principles of the normal and the pathological" rather than health (Foucault 1973, 36). In the words of Ivan Illich (1976, 53), "in every society, medicine, like law and religion, defines what is normal, proper, or desirable." Although the exercise of power in Iran is beyond the scope of this book, I will consider the case of those who use/

have used substances in prison or treatment centers, demonstrating there is no departure from the prevalent modality of power manifested through repression and destruction. Medicalization emerges as yet another form of criminalization.

Zola defined medicalization as a "process whereby more and more of everyday life has come under medical dominion, influence and supervision" (1983, 295). Or, as Conrad (1992, 211) states, "Medicalization consists of defining a problem in medical terms, using medical language to describe a problem, adopting a medical framework to understand a problem, or using a medical intervention to 'treat' it." According to Conrad (1992), medicalization can be observed at three levels: conceptual, institutional, and interactional. On the conceptual level, medical vocabulary is borrowed to define or "order" the issue which is not necessarily with the involvement of medical treatments or medical personnel. On the institutional level, institutions adopt the medical approach to resolve issues. Medical experts become gatekeepers for the benefits that are provided to the institutions adopting a medical approach. On this level, nonexperts oversee accomplishing daily work, while on the interactional level physicians are involved in routine activities and define an issue as medical or treat a "social" issue based on medical prescriptions.

Criminalization is the prevailing approach in Iran. To the extent that medicalization is involved in the treatment process as an auxiliary tool, I intend to warily articulate in this book that medicalization occurs more on the conceptual level, which is traceable in NA, rather than on the institutional and interactional levels.

Thus, I consider NA as a critical case of medicalization—a separate chapter discusses the lived experiences of NA members. According to Flyvbjerg (2006, 230), critical case is one of the strategies used for the selection of samples "to achieve information that permits logical deductions of the type. If this is (not) valid for this case, then it applies to all (no) cases." Almost all the harm reduction/treatment/recovery centers in Iran are practicing medicalization as a supplement to criminalization. The failure of law enforcement and policies related to addiction and drugs in Iran is not novel; references to medicalization despite prevailing criminalization have led even nongovernmental drug treatment organizations to become part of a vicious cycle. If criminalization discourse considers people who use substances as "criminals" and this stigma penetrates even the culture of NA, which has "no affiliation with any organizations outside of NA including governments, religions, law enforcement groups, or medical and psychiatric associations,"[4] then it is likely the same problem exists in other drug treatment centers. Alternatively, if humanizing, blameless, optimistic, and efficient methods are ineffective under the banner of a "medical ideology"[5] in NA, then it is unlikely they would succeed in any other case.

This book does not aim to criticize medicalization or assess damage dealt under its banner. Rather, it aims to depict the lived experiences of those who use substances in the context of the seemingly conflicting discourses of criminalization and medicalization in the Islamic Republic of Iran. Governing and controlling the bodies and lives of people who use substances was expanded from prison to the treatment, recovery, and harm reduction centers decades ago in Iran. Punishing the bodies of people who use substances is the most latent part of the medicalization process. Still, there is not even "a trace of holding on the bodies;" direct punishment is employed under the banner of medicine, which explicitly targets individuals' bodies and involves particular rituals, from street arrest and forceful escort by family and drug treatment centers employees to detoxification (Foucault 1979, 15). People who use substances become locked in endless and ineffective rituals, which degrade and isolate them instead of enhancing their lives. One interviewee, who had used substances for more than fifteen years, could name more than thirty governmental and NGO treatment centers that failed to deliver on their promise of a drug-free lifestyle.

---

4. From https://na.org/?ID=PR-index.

5. Conrad (1992, 216) distinguished "three types of medical social control: medical ideology, collaboration, and technology. Simply stated, medical ideology imposes a medical model primarily because of accrued social and ideological benefits; in medical collaboration doctors assist (usually in an organizational context) as information providers, gatekeepers, institutional agents, and technicians; medical technology suggests the use for social control of medical technological means, especially drugs, surgery, and genetic or other types of screening." However, he believes that they are overlapping categories and are found in combination with each other.

6   Life on Drugs in Iran

> I was frustrated and hopeless. None of those centers, from the most popular ones to the most hidden, illegal, and unpopular ones, worked. I was not the only one who was wandering among different camps for several years. I lost all I had, but none of those camps could help me.

Medicalization in Iran has not functioned as Foucault assumes (i.e., power/knowledge). Punishment is used instead of knowledge; "it is still necessary for the law to reach and manipulate the body of the convict" (Foucault 1979, 11) without keeping a distance; that is, in the proper way and based on strict rules. "A much higher aim" of treatment or recovery appears to be forgotten. One of the reports of the Iran Drug Control Headquarters (DCHQ) explicitly stated "what is happening in the drug treatment centers under the supervision of Welfare Organizations is just cutting the physical relation of addicts with drugs during their stay in the centers with no attention toward the causes of physical and phycological dependency on drugs . . ." (Madani 2011, 476). Fake medicalization acts as a mechanism of social control, a pseudo prison, and a combination of social issues, a job creation platform, and a profitable business that continues to target the bodies of people who use substances.

This book is not about the premodern or modern history of drugs and addiction in Iran. There are comprehensive and excellent works on this topic, including *The Pursuit of Pleasure: Drugs and Stimulants in Iranian History, 1500–1900* by Rudi Matthee and *E'tiyad Dar Iran* (Addiction in Iran) by Saeed Madani. This book does not aim to study politics and the state—the political structure of Iran and how it exercises power through drug politics is discussed in detail by Maziyar Ghiabi in his book *Drugs Politics: Managing Disorder in the Islamic Republic of Iran*. This book is also not a study of democracy in Iran, nor does it focus on the contested relations between the state and civil society in the context of drug politics—though Janne Bjerre Christensen has written an impressive book titled *Drugs, Deviancy and Democracy in Iran: The Intersection of State and Civil Society* on this issue. The present book is a supplement to this rich literature. While most of the existing scholarship concentrates on policies, politics, the state, and stakeholders, I will focus on the perceptions of the people who are forgotten and most vulnerable to the impacts of the state's policies. By focusing exclusively on the state and politics, it becomes much more challenging to discern how those who use or have used substances survive under these regimes. Although there are several reports by physicians, medical experts, and psychologists regarding drug addictions and drug treatments in Iran, as Ghiabi (2019, 5) states, most are "epidemiological studies prioritizing narrow quantitative methods at the expense of qualitative, sociological and historical approaches."

The dearth of scholarly works regarding the lived experiences of people who use drugs in Iran inspired me to write this book.

This book will explore the challenges of the lives of people who use substances in Iran and face severe punishments, but at the same time are provided with a comprehensive "public health" system. While most Muslim countries and some Western states still do not espouse welfare-oriented measures such as harm reduction centers, Iran has established several harm reduction centers nationwide through the welfare system for those who use substances (Ghiabi 2018). Despite prisons in Iran being replete with people who use substances, the state continues to showcase its so-called medicalization and scientific drug policies. The disguise of medicalization and modifying the title from "crime" to "disease" is like milking a ram. At any given moment in history, various meanings are attached to addiction, drugs, and people who use substances. Although this book briefly covers different approaches toward the topic of drugs, its main purpose transcends policies and politics; it is about people who become victims of what is called "transformation," even though it is ultimately no more than a new disguise. My aim is to investigate how people who use and have used substances wander among prisons, treatment centers, and NGOs and are criminalized, medicalized, and marginalized as the system attempts to normalize them.

One might assume that, because of amendments in drug policies and the consideration of people who use substances as patients rather than criminals, addiction is stigma free. Even though prison is much more stigmatized than drug treatment centers in Iran, people who use substances

8 Life on Drugs in Iran

are perceived as outcasts in prison and in drug treatment centers.[6] Some people, by referring to criminalization and medicalization, might believe there is no single, clear-cut approach to drug addiction in Iran. However, I strongly believe there is criminalization in its various forms. The remainder are merely its converse, inconsistent shades and types.

If we express the same idea in Foucault's language, there is no distinction between prisons and treatment programs, as both are a part of a disciplining project, while Christensen (2011, 45) finds "that normalizing drug users through a rehabilitation programme is a better idea than incarcerating them as criminals." I partly agree with the Foucauldian ideology that there is no difference between these two institutions. I also believe that neither prison nor rehabilitation programs in Iran are disciplining the individual. Although I would like to find Foucauldian rationalities in Iran, the reality is instead "regimes of fabrication" as opposed to "regimes of truth." The statuses of people who use substances in Iran remain unclear, and there is a paucity of literature regarding the impact of blurred boundaries between what constitutes a patient and a criminal in the lives of people who use substances. The fact is that neither law enforcement nor health organizations aim to normalize, rehabilitate, or optimize the life of people who use/used substances. Although Christensen (2011, 148) states that these organizations "tend to pull in opposite directions," I believe they are two sides of the same coin. Treatment policies contribute to the spread of morally acceptable language toward drug addiction in Iran—but the essence is the same and is hidden under the notions of treatment and medicalization.

The assumption of medicalization is refuted by several facts. First, illegal drugs are prevalent in prison and in some cases are higher quality than those purchased on the street, while Methadone Maintenance Treatment (MMT) is being practiced with the objective of decreasing the demand for heroin injection. The rapid growth of private and state-run rehabilitation

---

6. It is not my intention to deny the role of "Narcotics Anonymous" in decreasing the stigma attached to people who use or have used substances. However, the same phenomenon, manipulated by the crime-oriented approach, is at play.

and treatment clinics nationwide where coercive treatment methods prevail is another. An increasing focus on treatment and rehabilitation while people who are unwilling to seek treatment are still considered criminals is also important. Drug treatment camps also have more in common with punitive than rehabilitative institutions, as Alizade et al. (2020) state. The lack of governmental financial support, economic crises, and high rates of unemployment in Iranian society make these so-called treatment camps job-creation platforms and a profitable enterprise. Addiction has become a profitable business not only for state-run treatment organizations but also for the private sector. According to Rahimi Movaghar, cited by Madani (2011, 472):

> The private sector instantaneously entered the addiction field without any supervision, monitoring, and restraints as it happened with barbershops or beauty shops. Even Ministry of Health did not consider the treatment centers as a place which is supposed to be monitored and surveilled . . . Addiction became a business and a market for the physicians not only in Iran but also in other countries. However, it happens in Iran in an extreme way to this extent that addicts are victims of physicians . . . none of those treatments work since there is no follow-up process [of people admitted into the treatment centers] or monitoring [of treatment centers].

As I was speaking with one of my interviewees in a governmental women's treatment center, a manager who had no preliminary information about addiction joined our discussion and spoke sarcastically about my hesitation regarding the scientific treatment methods in the center. She stated:

> We have a very professional psychologist who is an expert on addiction and drugs. She deliberately and intentionally makes herself dependent on ice eating to better understand the addiction experience. She started to eat ice every day to the point where she could not survive without eating ice. She put herself deliberately into situations in which it was challenging to get ice. After a couple of months, she decided to quit eating ice. She explained how difficult it was to get rid of the ice eating habit.

10   Life on Drugs in Iran

She was really professional. She put herself in this situation to understand addicts; otherwise, she could not help patients in the center. If this not a scientific method for treating addiction, then what is it?

Struggling with the Nuances of Power

The information I collected in this study is based on participant observation and interviews conducted with NGO managers, treatment center managers, prisoners, people who use and have used substances, and NA members.[7] This book was composed from research gathered over nine years. My previous studies surrounding prison systems provided me with an in-depth understanding of contradictory policies and strategies to deal with various social issues that do not go beyond mere declarations. Most of those who have been interviewed[8] were like a "living encyclopedia;" they had a wealth of experiences due to considerable time spent in various institutions, from prison, NA, and state-run treatment centers to illegal treatment centers. Although I did not gain access to the prison in 2017, I traveled to various cities (i.e., Isfahan, Tehran, Kerman, and Mazandaran; see figure 1) and gained access to a variety of governmental organizations (e.g., state-run treatment camps[9]) and NGOs (e.g., NA, rehabilitation centers, and night drop-in centers). I was also able to speak to a myriad of participants with long and short incarceration experiences. In addition to maximizing variation and saturating categories, gaining access to the harm reduction/treatment/recovery centers (governmental or nongovernmental), and interviewing managers and employees of those organizations

---

7. I utilized Grounded Theory (GT) in my research. The field work was approved by Memorial's Research Ethics Board and was performed in accordance with TCSP (Canada's Tri-Council Policy Statement: Ethical Conduct for Research Involving Humans).

8. The participants consisted of thirty-eight men and fifty-two women aged ten to sixty-five years.

9. According to the manager of one of the state-run camps, "whenever the police collect drug users in the street and there are no available beds in the compulsory camps, they are sent here. However, most are sent to compulsory camps designed as an alternative to prison."

1. Map of Iran

in different cities, persuaded me of the prevalence of criminalization across all addiction programs and led me to choose NA as a critical case of medicalization.

Accessing the field of study in this case was not just about finding the most appropriate and informative locations and initiating the interview process; I needed to confront the dominant moral order in the society. Interviewing NA members was a challenging experience, especially as far as women who still struggled with the stigma and shame of addiction are concerned, since those women did not participate in the public NA meetings. Instead, through a snowball effect, some participants encouraged other potential participants or their friends to take part. Recruiting women in nongovernmental treatment centers was even more challenging. To build trusting relationships, I got involved in their daily activities such as book reading, cooking, caring for their children, and educational classes. As I was involved and engaged in the participants' daily lives while I collected data and was constantly immersed in the field of study, I was occasionally mistaken for a person who uses or had used substances. While

12 Life on Drugs in Iran

I was helping one participant prepare a dinner in the night drop-in center, the assistant manager arrived and started a conversion with me about the rules I should follow if I wanted to stay in the center and the accommodations that would be provided during my stay. On another occasion, after a long discussion with an NA member who was a manager of an NGO, he concluded, "Of course, you are a researcher, but I'm one hundred percent sure that you are an NA member as well."

Studying the lived experiences of women who use substances was far more constrained and sensitive than studying their male counterparts. It was less challenging to conduct interviews with high-status managers in the welfare organization regarding drug policy or, as Christensen (2011, 18) states, with "the major policymakers in the field of drug policy, such as the Drug Control Headquarters and the Ministry of Health" than it was to access women's treatment camps and conduct interviews.

Women who use substances in Iranian society violate several social taboos. I remember a day in the summer of 2017 when, after negotiating with several academics, NGO managers, and NA members, I found the approximate location of two state-run, women's treatment centers. To access at least one, I needed to complete a formal procedure, which I immediately knew would not yield satisfactory results. Nevertheless, I scheduled an appointment with one of the directors in a welfare organization who could provide official access to drug treatment camps. When I raised the subject, she explicitly denied the existence of the camp and spoke to her belief that my research is morally wrong and might spread rumors regarding women who use substances. She attempted to convince me to modify my research objectives to something neutral, such as children and youth studies. Before even hearing a brief explanation of my research, but immediately after hearing the words "women and addiction," she interrupted me. Evidently, she felt offended by my research topic. One of her colleagues in the room joined the discussion, asking personal questions regarding my previous studies, age, marital status, phone number, and address. Their reactions and beliefs about women who use substances were supported by the institutional power of the organization and the state. Thus, they felt that they were on a morally higher ground with justification to impose their beliefs on me. Had I not left the room, they would have asked another colleague to join them for further "persuasion."

This conversation happened exactly two days after I had identified the two women's treatment camps. I took my chance to attempt to gain permission by negotiating with the manager of the camp in person. The manager of the state-run women's treatment center was an NA member and, as I expected, did not initially disclose its exact location. The center was in a marginal region with no signboard. Exactly one street next to the women's treatment center, there was a treatment center for men with a large signboard at the top of the front door, exhibiting the name of the institution in bold letters. Initially I confused this institution with the one I was searching for; however, I quickly recognized it as a center for men. I asked the manager whether he was aware of any treatment center for women in the neighborhood, but he denied any knowledge of such. Finally, when I managed to find the women's treatment center, a guard in the adjacent kiosk asked why I was there and subsequently called the manager of the center. In this moment, I realized that the manager had misunderstood my situation—she had assumed I use substances and was seeking treatment services, and this was the reason why she had agreed to disclose the address at the very last moment. Nonetheless, after I insisted, she agreed to meet me. I had a long meeting with the manager in her room in the middle of the camp yard, attempting to convince her to grant me permission to access the field. I had no success. She perceived me as a troublemaker and thought that my research would cause challenges and result in the camp being shut down by authorities. She thought our cooperation regarding people who use substances would do nothing but lead to my arrest (*saret ro to zendan zire abb mikonan*).

The women's drug treatment centers are usually located outside city limits in depressed regions with high crime rates. This was the case for a night drop-in center, which was open from 7:00 p.m. to 7:00 a.m. For two weeks, I used taxis to transport me there at 8:00 p.m. and return at 2:00 a.m. Nearly all the taxi drivers treated me with suspicion after reading the address of the center. All of them had heard about it—and all of them were wary. One day, a taxi driver told me with concern, "It is not good for you to go to those types of places. Be careful, you are young. Where is your *mard* (husband, brother, or father)? If I were your family, I would not let you go into that place. Go back home, girl. If you want, I will take you back." Yet, returning from the center at 2:00 a.m. was the most challenging part. All center personnel wanted me to inform them of my safe return home. Each time I exited the center door, my taxi drivers gawped with open mouths and wide eyes, wondering what business I could possibly have there at that time of night. Even traveling to the treatment center, which I would visit from morning until afternoon, was challenging. I needed to pass through gatherings of people who use substances and dealers on the street—and each time, one of the center's patients accompanied me home. She told me, "Nahid, how do you dare come here alone? You don't have family in this city. Please go back to your city, Nahid. I know that you've got used to this situation after ten days, but I'm so worried about you. Those days that you want to come here, I tell my friends to pray for you. Nahid, give me all your questions and just go home. I'll ask all of them for you and give back the answers to you."

It is these challenges that I examine in this book, which is divided into five chapters. In this introduction, I define medicalization and how it is practiced in Iranian addiction and recovery centers. I also discuss the challenges and difficulties associated with conducting research in Iran, especially research on sensitive and critical topics. This includes my extensive efforts and attempts to gain access to the field.

The first chapter briefly articulates the history of addiction and drug policies, as well as modifications and amendments to anti-narcotic laws in the Islamic Republic of Iran. Clearly this chapter does not trace all developments in Iranian drug and addiction policies and programs, which is beyond the scope of this book. Rather, chapter 1 provides a brief overview of the history of drug policies in Iran as they relate to this publication.

Pathways to the onset and development of addiction are discussed in chapter 2. Although individual factors such as biology and cognitive behavior are involved in the development of addiction, social factors also play a pivotal role. A dysfunctional family, living in a criminal neighborhood, and deviant peers are among the most consistent and influential factors in modeling or encouraging use.

Chapter 3 depicts the prison subculture with particular attention to drug/addiction-related incidents, shedding light on the lived experiences of drug-related criminals in prison through six categories: (1) Unstable Pyramid, (2) Captive as a Society, (3) Battle Zone, (4) Hegemony of Drug-Related Networks, (5) Recriminalization and Re-Drugization, and (6) Two Sides of the Same Coin. However, a pathway to addiction has been addressed at the very beginning of this section. This chapter also examines the experiences of people in state-run compulsory camps and compulsory labor camps run under medicalization (Article 16 of the Anti-Narcotic Law) and criminalization (Article 42 of the Anti-Narcotic Law) approaches, respectively.

Chapter 4 is focused on NA as a critical case of the medical-oriented approach to addiction. Four categories are discussed with regard to NA's ideology and principles according to the lived experiences of NA members: (1) Horizontal Network; (2) Restricted and Exclusive Trust; (3) Constructing and Reconstructing Identity; and (4) Gender-Based Reintegration. The objective of the chapter, rather than to simply articulate narratives of NA members, is to give voice to the people who have been experiencing life under criminalization, wandering from treatment camp to camp without success. Even in NA, they struggle with challenges such as restricted and exclusive trust, a continuous process of identity reconstruction, and powerlessness, which reveals the invisible impact of a criminalization-oriented dominant approach on their life. This chapter also covers the experiences of people in night drop-in and NGO treatment centers.

In chapter 5, I introduce contested identity as one of the critical components of the lives of people who use substances, either in prison or in NA. The identity of people who use substances fluctuates between that of a patient in recovery in NA to a criminal in prison; it shifts rapidly but is restricted exclusively to predefined identities, which are also context dependent. Although in the modern world, identity is also shifting, fluid, plural, and contested, people who use substances can be considered a manifestation of the contested identity. They experience the most brutal transition process from a simple and uncontested identity to a plural and contested identity because of exclusion from society and being trapped within unnecessary struggles. Their freedom will appear to be restricted in those circumstances. The contested identity of people who use substances in Iran results less from shifting modernity than from inherent contradictions between criminalization and medicalization. As a result, they are shifting from predefined identities of dangerous criminals to vulnerable patients, which decreases the chance of reaching a balance between these identities. By neither rejecting traditional perceptions toward drugs and drug addiction nor adopting the modern approaches, Iran creates a situation in which people who use substances have "sick criminal" identities attached to them in prison and in treatment centers.

1

History

A Journey from Opium to Heroin and Methadone

Drug use is not novel in Iran. The history of drugs began with opium (*afyun* or *taryak*), which was introduced through the campaigns of Alexander the Great and perceived as a "panacea against all kinds of diseases" (Matthee 2005, 98). Although the line between medical and recreational use is unclear, there is no doubt that opium was in widespread use as a euphoric in the Safavid period (1501–1722). Generally, opium touched all segments of society, from the ruling elite to ordinary citizens, and it became "a normative element of life in Iran" (Ghiabi 2019, 39) because there was no religious or legal prohibition, and it was affordable to most. As Tavernier (cited by Matthee 2005, 113) states, "It was hard to find a man in Iran who was not addicted to any of these [opium and other hallucinatory] substances."

During the Safavid reign, there were even particular places designated for opium consumption, which were called "*koknar khaneh*" (Madani 2011, 142). In 1729, a restriction on the cultivation and consumption of opium was issued by Shah Tahmasb, and this was followed by a similar restriction imposed by Agha Muhammad Khan in the Qajar reign (1796). However, these restrictions had no immediate impact on opium consumption (Matthee 2005). In early Qajar, the cultivation of opium in Iran was limited and mostly occurred in Yazd province, where the production yielded between 8,200 and 9,825 kilograms of opium in 1837. However, in the nineteenth century, the cultivation of opium was no longer based on domestic consumption, as it began to play a crucial role in the

18   Life on Drugs in Iran

Iranian economy. Opium exports increased from 42,000 pounds[1] in 1859 to 875,000 pounds in 1914 and grew to 1,100,000 pounds in 1925 (Matthee 2005; Ghiabi 2019). Opium consumption and trade were once again banned by Mirza-Abd al-Wahhab Khan Shirazi, a governor of Khurasan, in 1881. The strictest restrictions on opium cultivation and consumption were subsequently issued after the Constitutional Revolution in 1911.

The Constitutionalists considered addiction to be one of the most serious social and political issues facing Iran. Thus, the law of Opium Limitation (*Qanun-e Tahdid-e Tariyak*) was issued by Parliament in 1911, giving people who used opium a seven-year period to quit (Madani 2011). Also, according to the 1911 law, the government became the main distributor of opium in the country through the creation of a quota system (*sahmiyeh*), which delivered specific amounts of opium to people who used substances. This was followed by restrictions on the production, trade, and manufacturing of opiates in 1913, and then restrictions on the cultivation and consumption of opium in 1919. Despite these prohibitions and restrictions, in 1939, more than forty percent of residents of Mazandaran claimed to use opium (Matthee 2005). In 1943, more than ten percent of the population in Iran used opium, and 1.5 million out of the population of 19 million people claimed to be using substances (Christensen 2011).

During the Pahlavi dynasty (1925–79), especially amid the reign of Mohammad Reza Shah (1941–79), poppy cultivation was banned, heavier penalties for drug-related crimes were issued, and several detoxification programs were implemented (Christensen 2011). From 1974 to 1977, several detoxification programs operated in Iran, providing people who used substances with methadone treatment and opium coupons to help them cope with the detoxification process. These programs were eventually replaced by state-run compulsory treatment camps after the Revolution (Nissaramanesh et al. 2005; Alam-Mehrjerdi et al. 2015).

In 1979, the Islamic Revolution in Iran brought to power the radical conservative Islamists under the leadership of the supreme leader Ayatollah Ruhollah Khomeini, with a strict anti-drug agenda. The leader of the

---

1. One pound is equivalent to 0.45 kilogram.

Islamic Revolution in Iran announced that the consumption and trafficking of illicit drugs in the new Islamic Republic of Iran was opposed to the rules of Islam, the revolutionary values, as well as a direct result of the influence of Western culture and consequently should be prohibited.[2] Thus in 1980, along with the total prohibition and eradication of opiates and poppy crops, the purification of people who use substances through massive waves of arrests and executions was undertaken by the "hanging judge" Ayatollah Khalkhali, the head of the anti-narcotic campaign (Ghiabi 2019; Christensen 2011; Abrahamian 1999). Despite the prevalence of opium consumption among Iranians since the fifteenth century (especially among elderly men), the pervasiveness of drug abuse among younger groups across all social classes was referred to as a "social plague" after 1979 (Christensen 2011, 122). After the revolution, drug addiction began to be considered a crime against the state, religion, and national security for the first time (Ghiabi 2019). However, in the aftermath of the war, according to Varzi (2006, 160), "Even the most religious of war veterans have become opium and heroin addicts. Too frustrated, depressed, and angry, and not strong enough to take the correct mystical path to self-obliteration, they now opt for drugs."

The Iran-Iraq War (1980–88), together with the conflict in Afghanistan following the Soviet invasion, made Iran the most important destination for importing drugs from the world's leading opium poppy producer, Afghanistan, despite the harsh criminal penalties imposed by the revolutionary government for drug consumption and trafficking (Calabrese 2007). In 1980, Iran was involved in a war against Iraq, and also in a war on drugs.[3] According to the law on drugs in 1980, the possession of

---

2. It is not only the regime that associates drugs with the West; many of the participants in Mahdavi's (2007, 452) study about sexual behaviors of young people in contemporary Iran "believe that engaging in certain sexual behaviors or using certain substances is more 'Western' and perhaps more in style."

3. As one of the interlocutors in Molavis' (2002, 266) study, who was a *basij* (volunteer) and was sent to the eastern front to fight drug smugglers, recounted, "We had so many volunteers that I was not needed in the south and west, where the war was being fought. I was sent east to fight against drug smugglers. Many of the smugglers increased their operations

20   Life on Drugs in Iran

1 kilogram of opiates would result in a death penalty sentence. As Ghiabi (2019, 79) states, "Addiction, per se, was a criminal offence even without possession of drugs, and remained in the focus of legal debates up until the late 2010s." In 1983, in addition to incarceration, state-run treatment centers that mostly focused on detoxification with no medically assisted surveillance were established in fifteen cities. While the number of state-run treatment centers decreased from twenty-one in 1983 to seventeen in 1988, the number of patients increased from 2,987 to 28,175 (Madani 2011). From 1980 to 1989, thousands of people who used substances were sent to the prisons or compulsory camps (Nissaramanesh et al. 2005). In addition to being locked in prisons and treatment centers, people who used substances and lived in the street with a criminal history were arrested and sent to the islands in the south of Iran, surrounded by guards with no time allotted to quit their drug habit (Madani 2011). In the war on drugs, clerics were invited to enlighten people regarding the dangers of drugs. Also, as a component of anti-narcotic operations, the Islamic Revolutionary Guards arranged sites where "the morally deviant elements in the community, e.g., gamblers and drug dealers, were identified and isolated" (Bayat 1997, 92). Despite these measures, the number of people arrested related to drug crimes increased from 9,867 in 1979 to 92,046 in 1988 (Madani 2011, 252).

By the end of the war, during the Reconstruction Era of President Ayatollah Hashemi Rafsanjani (1989–97), the focus of the state was toward internal issues, including drugs, which were considered a crucial social problem along with unemployment and high living costs (Ghiabi 2019, 95). In 1988, an anti-narcotics agency, the Drug Control Headquarters (*setad-e mobarz-e ba mavad-e mokhader*), was established through the Anti-Narcotic Law to organize and coordinate all drug-related policies nationwide. According to the 1988 Anti-Narcotic Law, those who were convicted for the possession of more than five kilograms of opium or hashish and more than thirty grams of heroin, methadone, or morphine

---

because they thought we would be too occupied with the war. The Imam did not want us to forget our national duties to fight against drugs amid the chaos of the war."

were sentenced to death. The director of Iran Drug Control Headquarters (DCHQ), Mohammad Fellah, was a critical figure in the medicalization of addiction by emphasizing a medical approach rather than a punitive one. However, this vision of medicalization was not implemented until 1997, when the Expediency Council approved that people who use substances could be treated without punishment. Nevertheless, addiction was still a crime (Ghiabi 2019).

Under the shadow of the government's intentions toward privatization of some sections of economy, drug issues were also transformed. A wide range of private institutions assumed a significant role in the addiction field; as Ghiabi (2019, 97) states, "Private practices of cure and pseudo-treatment remained a vibrant sector of Iran's addiction para-medicine." The drug law in 1988 was still crime-oriented and emphasized supply reduction, and no substantial measures were taken toward demand or harm reduction. Furthermore, in early 1992, the NAJA or the Islamic Republic of Iran Law Enforcement Force were created by merging the *Shahrbani* (city police), the Gendarmerie, and the Islamic Revolutionary committee, which empowered the police to fight the country's war on drugs. As a result, the number of drug-related arrests increased from 396,986 in 1980–88 to 738,167 in 1989–96 (Madani 2011, 339).

In 1999, a radical change occurred in drug consumption. Afghanistan banned poppy cultivation, causing people who used substances to switch from opium to heroin because of the increased opium price (Ghiabi 2019). Thus, from 1999 onward, sharp increases in the availability of affordable heroin, heroin addiction, and heroin injection were recorded. Heroin ballooned addiction from the private to the public sphere (e.g., "men sleeping on park benches, drugged soldiers swaying their way through a public park, women beggars slumped over on the sidewalk with their children either doped and slugged across their shoulders [sic]"), which changed the perception of the Islamic paradise (Varzi 2006, 161). The Rapid Situation Assessment (RSA) estimated that in Iran there were 1.2 million people who use heroin and 800,000 who use recreational substances. According to the results of one of the representative nationwide surveys conducted in 2001, the number of people who use opium and heroin in the country was about 3.76 million (Calabrese 2007). According to Ghiabi (2018), other

22   Life on Drugs in Iran

than the cultural tendency of Iranians to use opium (opium has a long history of use for medical purposes and domestic consumption), methamphetamine (*shisheh*) and heroin have seen recent, rapid increases in use. In 2003, between 1.7 percent and 2.8 percent of Iranians were reportedly addicted to opium-based drugs, and Iran accounted for seventy-three percent of opium and twenty-five percent of heroin seizures[4] in the world (UNODC 2012). One of the consequences of heroin dependency and the rise in injecting drugs was an epidemic of HIV/AIDS, which disproportionately affected people who use harmful substances in prison, where a syringe that has been used thirty to forty times costs a fortune. In 2001, the number of people who inject drugs was between 200,000 and 300,000, and the number of people infected by HIV was 2,458, 74.8 percent of whom were injection drug users (Nissaramanesh et al. 2005).

The prevalence of opium use and heroin injection in Iran was an explicit sign of the failure and limits of law enforcement as an official policy to address drug issues, which paved the way toward adapting a new approach to addiction in 1994. Widespread critical arguments regarding the overemphasis on the supply reduction and a punitive approach became popular, which provided fertile soil for the introduction of harm reduction and treatment centers and shifting strategies from reducing drug use and production to reducing harm and from anti-trafficking activities to addressing drug-related issues of consumers. For instance, Mohammad Fellah, the DCHQ director, in a 1994 speech, clearly stated that execution and incarceration were not effective enough to address addiction issues in the country, especially with respect to those who were smuggling drugs and not major drug traffickers (Madani 2011).

The social and political atmosphere of Iran was transformed during the reformist government of Mohammad Khatami (1997–2005), which directly impacted the field of addiction and drug policy. The expansion of

---

4. In Canada, "although there had been an increase in heroin seizures from 2008 to 2009, seizures decreased considerably, from 213 kg in 2009 to 98 kg and cannabis herb seizures increased from 34 to 51 tons in 2010" (World Drug Report 2012, 29, 51).

civil society and constant interaction between the government and civic groups regarding social issues was a hallmark of Khatami's era. However, the failure of fundamental and consistent reforms became obvious even before his second term was over.

In the mid-1990s, compulsory therapeutic communities under government surveillance and using prison infrastructure offered nonstandardized treatments to people referred by a court order (Razzaghi et al. 1999). In the early 2000s, a discussion regarding methadone as an alternative to opium and heroin was raised by the medical community as a new strategy to address the crisis. Along with the development of NA with their twelve-step philosophy, outpatient centers that offered short-term detoxification using clonidine grew rapidly. However, the effectiveness of short-term detoxification treatments was questioned, and substitute long-term treatment programs were established (Nissaramanesh et al. 2005). In 1999, the first harm reduction clinic, called Persepolis NGO, was established by Bijan Nissaramanesh in Shiraz as an "underground needle exchange program," which also offered buprenorphine tablets (Buprenorphine Maintenance Treatment or BMT) from 1999–2001 and obtained a license from the Ministry of Health in 2001 (Nissaramanesh et al. 2005; Ghiabi 2019, 115). Iran is a pioneer in drug addiction treatment, legalizing harm reduction long before most Western countries. From 2000–2002, drop-in centers (DICs) were established in Tehran to provide people who use substances with harm reduction facilities, from clean needles to condoms and methadone maintenance treatment (MMT) (Alam-Mehrjerdi et al. 2015). Over the same period, Kamiar and Arash Alaei, two brothers and physicians, initiated harm reduction activities in Kermanshah and established a triangular clinic, which provided harm reduction materials, MMT, and facilities related to HIV/AIDS. By the mid-2000s, triangular clinics had been introduced into Iranian prisons as well, which was supported by the Khatami government. However, the dominance of punishment discourse over addiction and drug issues was undeniable, as law enforcement agencies were actively operating against the harm reduction centers' activities by arresting the patients. As the manager of one of the most important and oldest harm reduction centers explained:

I was shocked by these contradictory acts by the state regarding drug addicts. On the one side, people who use substances came to my center to receive their methadone, and on the other side, the police arrested them. Sometimes, I thought that the harm reduction centers were being used as a big trap for addicts to be arrested by police. One day, I was invited to the International Day of Anti-Narcotics ceremony, and the ceremony building was filled with soldiers and administrative officials. There were several speakers. One of the most astonishing and unfortunate parts of the ceremony was when they set fire to the illegal drugs that were seized by anti-narcotics police. Once this part of the ceremony was announced, I got scared and thought it might explode, since there were large amounts of illicit drugs to destroy. I sneakily left the campus and went across the hall. Suddenly, one of the soldiers asked me why I was leaving. I told him that I was scared, as there were a lot of drugs, which were going to be lit on fire, and I feared a possible explosion. He just laughed in my face and said, "Did you seriously think those are drugs that are going to be lit on fire? They are all straw. They never set fire to drugs. Those are funny games which are managed and controlled by the government."

Finally, in 2005, the bill for the "decriminalization of treatment of those suffering from narcotic drug abuse" was approved by President Mohammad Khatami's ministerial cabinet, and the Ministry of Health and the Ministry of Social Security were assigned to oversee the prevention, treatment, and harm reduction of drugs and addiction in Iran. This is not to say that drug addiction was no longer considered a crime in Iran, but rather a curable crime.

Under the populist government of Mahmud Ahmadinejad (2005–13), Iran witnessed widespread sociocultural and political changes. After a presidential election in 2009, the Green Movement (*Jonbesh-e Sabz*) and widespread protests against the state followed by mass arrest of protestors and house arrest of the movement's leaders, Mir Hossein Musavi and Mehdi Karroubi assumed office. Over this period, excessive international sanctions, lack of investments, and unsystematic and disorganized industrial policy resulted in the economic downturn, unemployment, poverty, and social inequality under the Ahmadinejad's administration

A Journey from Opium to Heroin and Methadone   25

(Khosravi 2008; Ghiabi 2019).[5] In this environment, the rate of drug addiction significantly increased, as well as criminality and prostitution. As Khosravi (2008, 8) states, "more optimistic young people seek remedy in emigration." In June 2006, based on International Monetary Fund (IMF) estimates, about 150,000 to 180,000 people left the country. In 2010, according to the Management and Planning Organization Weekly, 90 out of 125 Iranian students, winners of disciplinary Olympiads, were studying in the United States (Karimi and Gharaati 2013). As Reza Malekzadeh, a member of the Supreme Council of the Cultural Revolution of Iran, states in 2014, "because we lack the necessary research and development infrastructure; we cannot prevent them from leaving the country" (Mahmoudi 2021). Regarding culture and art, various cultural institutes were shut down or restricted and public musical performances were limited or mostly banned (Siamdoust 2017). In 2009, the Ministry of Health of the Islamic Republic of Iran released a statement regarding the prevalence of sadness and depression in the country, demanding happiness engineering (Behrouzan and Fischer 2014).

On top of this, not only drug consumption thrived in this new dimension, but also drug policy. In 2006, the appearance of methamphetamine (*shisheh*) as a colorless smoke changed the pattern of addiction in Iran. In less than four years, more than seventy percent of people who use substances also smoked *shisheh*, which energized users and diminished their need for food or sleep. Existing medical treatments did not meet even the needs of people who used heroin and opium due to the lack of scientifically sound approaches, medical experts, a follow-up process, and the dominance of punishment-oriented policies, not to mention absent treatment for those using industrial drugs (e.g., methamphetamine) and requiring psychological and psychiatric interventions (Ghiabi 2019). In 2010, the Anti-Narcotic Law was revised and Articles 15 and 16 provided for the rehabilitation and treatment of people who use substances. In

---

5. The participants of Khosravi's (2008, 128) study about the situation of young people in Iran complain that "due to lack of entertainment (*tafrih*), unemployment, and an uncertain future, depression is high among the youth, who tend toward delinquency."

other words, drug treatment centers and programs became legitimized, marking a clear distinction between people who use drugs with a genuine desire to quit and those unwilling to stop who are subsequently subject to arrest. The death penalty was also introduced for possessing thirty grams or more of methamphetamine.

According to Article 15, people who use substances are required to be admitted to governmental, nongovernmental, and private camps or treatment and harm reduction centers to quit. Those who are admitted to these organizations for treatment and receive an identification of treatment or harm reduction will be exempted from criminal sanctions if they do not relapse. Meanwhile, anyone who uses substances without any intention to seek treatment is considered a criminal. According to Article 16, those who use substances mentioned in Articles 4 and 8 and do not have an identification card mentioned in Article 15 will be kept in licensed state-run treatment or harm reduction centers for one to three months by court order. The length of stay can be extended for an additional three months via a report from the treatment center or judicial authority.

If an individual who used substances is willing to be treated under Article 15, they will be allowed to do so. Only those who do not show a desire to change are viewed as failures unworthy to be considered as needing help. Thus, they are considered criminals who deserve punishment. As Pitch (1995, 21) states:

> It now functions as a legitimation for incapacitation, as the criterion of classification within the prison system itself and between custodial strategies as such and the policies of "soft" control . . . It functions as a residual category: all that which is not amenable to treatment or rehabilitation is therefore dangerous. Although the war on drugs has appeared to change its direction toward cultivating, distributing, and trafficking, it still targets people who use substances through Article 16 and its "purifying plans."

As a result of Iranian drug-law reforms in 2010, people using substances and living on the street are now regularly arrested by the police and sent to compulsory camps, which resemble prisons.

People who use substances are in fact still criminals, unless they have an identification card from the treatment center, in which case they fall under the category of a "patient criminal" (Ghiabi 2019). Despite legitimizing treatment and harm reduction centers in Iran, drug addiction remains a target of stigmatization and punishment. There is also no guarantee that those who seek harm reduction materials other than MMT or detoxification (i.e., clean needles) are exempt from prosecution. As discussed earlier, medical intervention is another branch of criminalization and the crime-oriented, punitive approach.

Shortly after the 2010 amendment, or even before that, the therapeutic police took charge and responsibility for collecting people using substances and living on the street, admitting them to the state-run compulsory camps. These camps are characterized by the excessive use of physical violence that is not humanitarian nor medicalized, but rather security-focused and criminalized. Other than state-run camps, private treatment camps also exist. They are managed by private organizations, charities, and associations and are funded through donations from families, members' fees, and welfare organizations. These institutions recruit people in recovery and NA members and provide the clients with detoxification services, twelve-step programs (i.e., NA), and therapists. Private camps target lower–middle class users referred on a voluntary basis and have negotiable fees.

In 2005, a total of 946 treatment and recovery centers (201 state-run and 745 from the private sector) were established, admitting 28,679 and 154,010 persons, respectively. Still, the large number of patients who returned to the centers after recovery is undeniable (Alizade et al. 2020). In 2007, there were 51 government treatment centers, 457 private centers, and 26 transition centers in Iran (Calabrese 2007). By 2009, according to the Drug Control Headquarters (2009), there were 1,596 treatment centers, 337 government facilities, and 1,232 nongovernmental facilities, which provided services for about 643,516 people. In 2011, there were 2,774 governmental and nongovernmental treatment and harm reduction camps in Iran, 88 percent of which were NGOs and just 12 percent of which were state-run institutes. In 2013, the legal treatment centers, under the supervision of the Ministry of Health, Welfare Organization, and Prison Organization, admitted 76,500 people (Alizade et al. 2020).

28   Life on Drugs in Iran

Not all treatment centers and camps in Iran are legal; a growing number of drug treatment camps have no legal status. Although they do not offer proper treatment supervision, they are absorbing large numbers of users who seek treatment. Reportedly, there are 400 illegal camps in Tehran, 294 illegal camps in Isfahan, and 50 illegal camps in Arak. According to Ghiabi (2018), despite several notifications of the state regarding the closure of illegal camps nationwide, most treatment camps in Iran still do not have a license from the Welfare Organization.[6] However, families of those who use drugs usually prefer to call the illegal camps' personnel instead of the police to collect family member who use substances from their home and transport them to the camp sites for treatment, even if this involves violence and beatings,[7] since the alternative involves criminal charges and dishonorable consequences in the community and neighborhood. As one of the NA recovering members and the most important weekly NA representative in one of the prisons, stated:

> One day when I was high on heroin, my mother called the police to arrest me. She thought that prison might make a good person of me and force me to quit drugs. The police arrested me that day and sentenced me to five years of incarceration. My mother made a big mistake in her life, as she put me in the most dangerous place for drug addicts (prison). Also, all the neighbours since then do not talk with my family because the police arrested me that day. You know, there are several parents who just call the camps and give them a bit of money to forcefully take their child from home and get them clean, but my mother was a fool. She ruined her own life and mine as well.

This is also an affordable option for low-income families who are seeking drug treatment. Additionally, the personnel and workers of the illegal treatment centers had often recovered in the camp and were recruited by

6. In this sense, the term "extra-legal," i.e., outside of the legal framework, may be more appropriate.

7. This result has been paralleled with some parts of the film titled "Life and a Day," which was directed by Saeed Roustayi in 2004; https://www.imdb.com/title/tt5460658/.

the manager as social workers. Thus, people in recovery who do not have any position as ordinary citizens in society can enhance their status by being employed in the camps. However, the treatment strategies applied in the illegal camps are controversial, as they include "*kotak-darmani* ('beating-treatment'), *ab-darmani* ('water-treatment'), *sag-darmani* ('dog treatment') and *zan-gir-darmani* ('chain-treatment')" (Ghiabi 2019). According to participants who were recruited in the illegal camps, beatings are the fundamental strategy used to control and manage camps, especially when new patient arrive. As one of the participants in a recovery camp noted:

> The only way to control them in the first days of detoxication was beating. The manager of the camp just beat them and yelled at them; otherwise, they were out of control.

The rapid growth of illegal camps in Iran is considered a double-edged sword, providing people in recovery with job opportunities while also subjecting them to unprofessional treatment strategies. In addition to state-run, private, and illegal treatment organizations in Iran, nongovernmental organizations with various philosophies and methods of action have grown dramatically in the field of addiction treatment and are mostly run by people who have used substances. However, the cycle of addiction treatment, harm reduction, and recovery does not function properly. It is characterized by lack of facilities and medical expertise on addiction. According to the Drug Control Headquarters, about one hundred nongovernmental treatment organizations are active in the addiction field and provide facilities for ninety thousand people nationwide (Christensen 2011).

Despite all these applied measures and the growing number of governmental, NGO, private, and illegal treatment centers, the number of individuals incarcerated for drug-related offences has risen sharply, from 101,801 people in 1993 to 204,385 in 2010 and 217,851 in 2014. As Ghiabi (2019, 11) states, "The case of Iran, in particular, provides a paradigm of what has come to be known as the 'War on Drugs,' in a political and cultural setting that has been characterised, by most of the area studies literature, by other investigations and scholarly questions." The clashes with

30   Life on Drugs in Iran

armed drug traffickers have been referred to as a "full-scale war" by the former foreign minister (1997–2005) Kamal Kharazzi (Calabrese 2007). It has been well documented that approximately sixty percent of Iranian prisoners are incarcerated due to drug-related crimes; over 80,000 drug-related offenders were arrested in 2000, and this number increased to 314,268 in 2007 (Calabrese 2007; Nissaramanesh et. al 2005).

Despite some "relaxing of political and cultural atmosphere" under the presidential term of Hasan Rouhani (2013–21) the social and economic crisis remained unchanged (Hunter 2014, 254; Ghiabi 2019). In 2015, the rate of unemployment, based on data from the Statistical Center of Iran, reached twenty to thirty percent in most provinces (Zimmt 2018). In 2017, as a result of economic hardships and significant increases in fuel prices, nationwide anti-government protests struck government. The protests were considered the largest challenge to the existing regime since the Green Movement. Less than two years before Rouhani's presential term ended, several incidents exacerbated the ongoing crisis in 2020. About fifty-six people were killed in the burial procession of Ghasem Soleimani, a top Iranian general, who was killed by a US air strike. Soon after, missiles launched by the Iranian Revolutionary Guard, reportedly in error, destroyed a Ukrainian International Airline flight, with 176 lives lost.

Meanwhile, in the field of drugs, Iranian forces seized 807 tonnes of various narcotics and psychotropic substances in 2018 alone. Statistics show that about 5.4 percent of Iranians aged fifteen to sixty-four used drugs in 2017 (Radio Farda 2019), and the increasing rate of addiction parallels a surge in the number of prisoners and of individuals sentenced to the death penalty. According to Iran Human Rights (2016, 16), "more than 2,990 people were executed on drug offences between 2010 and 2016."[8]

---

8. Article 8 in the Anti-Narcotic Law of the Islamic Republic of Iran: "Anyone who imports, exports, distributes, produces, deals in, keeps or stores, conceals and carries (or transports) heroin, morphine, cocaine and other chemical derivatives of morphine or cocaine shall be sentenced to the following punishments, taking into account the amount of said drugs: (1) Up to five centigrams, a fine in the amount of five hundred thousand to one million rials in cash plus twenty to fifty lashes; (2) More than five centigrams to one gram, a fine in the amount of two million to six million rials in cash plus thirty to seventy

A Journey from Opium to Heroin and Methadone   31

Despite the efforts of the Iranian government to reduce drug-related crime rates, the statistics indicate a crisis.

However, the spark of criminal justice reform began. In 2016, UN Human Rights Commissioner Zeid Ra'ad Al Hussein stated: "Given the broadening recognition in Iran that the death penalty does not deter drug crime and that anti-narcotics laws need to be reformed, I call on Iran to take the important first step of instituting a moratorium on the use of the death penalty" (United Nations News 2016). Deputy Head of the Judiciary for Social Affairs, Mohammad Baqer Olfat, also stated "[t]he truth is, the execution of drug smugglers has had no deterrent effect . . . We have fought full-force against smugglers according to the law, but unfortunately we are experiencing an increase in the volume of drugs trafficked to Iran, the transit of drugs through the country, the variety of drugs, and the number of people who are involved in it" (Reuters 2016). Drug trafficking laws were amended in 2018, and as a result, the threshold for the death penalty for drug possession cases increased, and pending death sentences for most inmates were reviewed or even commuted (Nikpour 2018). Iran has had a long history of struggling with drugs and addiction over the period of reconstruction by putting the private sector and family in charge and by affording opportunities to the civil groups to deal with the dilemma over the reformist era; as Ghiabi (2019, 14) states, by "outsourcing of drug control treatment and punishment to non-state, grassroots agents" during the populist government of Ahmadinejad. Undoubtedly, efforts have been dominated by crime-oriented policy and the 2013–21 presidential term of Hassan Rouhani, a "moderate and pragmatic politician," was no exception.

---

lashes; (3) More than one gram up to four grams, a fine in the amount of eight million to twenty million rials in cash plus two to five years of imprisonment and thirty to seventy lashes; (4) More than four grams up to fifteen grams a fine in the amount of twenty million to forty million rials in cash, plus five to eight years of imprisonment and thirty to seventy-four lashes; (5) More than fifteen up to thirty grams, a fine in the amount of forty million to sixty million rials fine in cash, plus ten to fifteen years of imprisonment and thirty and seventy-four lashes; (6) More than thirty grams, death penalty and confiscation of property excepting the normal living costs for the family of the convicted."

2

Accursed Pathway

Although the primary functions of family are the socialization and supervision of individuals, family can also be a facilitator of crime. In other words, families characterized by a history of excessive substance use, criminal history, physical and psychological violence, and poverty are known, crime-facilitating conditions. These circumstances often compel individuals toward the addiction pathway. Several studies (Willis and Rushforth 2003; Javdani et al. 2011; Dalley 2002) have emphasized that family problems are a key turning point to deviance and concluded that the family can be a facilitator of crime. In these studies, most participants were constant witnesses of conflict among family members. Some left home due to abusive and aggressive fathers and constant beatings. For instance, a twenty-eight-year-old participant in recovery chose to live on the street over living with her family to escape her subjugation to repeated physical and psychological violence inflicted by her father.

> My father has mental issues, and he was very religious. He did not accept the new lifestyle at all. He always beat me, and my mother was too weak to stand up against him. I left home occasionally, and my friends who smoked cigarettes sheltered me. Those friends became my life. Despite being beaten by my father every time I smoked drugs, I did not give up. I felt peace with my friends. I didn't want to be at my home anymore. (Female participant, began using drugs at age twelve)

Some participants did not receive even basic support from their parents (e.g., physical affection or discussing their problems and personal issues). In fact, their unengaged families, characterized by weak monitoring skills, especially among men, pushed them to use illicit drugs. The participants suffered from the unresponsiveness and unsupportiveness of their parents, which they called "cold parenting" and "careless parenting." One of the youngest participants of this study had four sisters, all of whom had a drug-free lifestyle—unlike their father. The father had been using substances ever since the participant could remember and was one of her most formative drug use influences. She was the last child of their family, and all her sisters were married before she got to know them. She said:

> My mother did not even know how old I was, or which grade I had to register for in school. One of our neighbours came to our home on the first day of school and told my mother that she would have to register at school. My mother answered: "How old is she?" It does not matter for her that I am using heroin or methamphetamine or drinking too much alcohol. She knows everything about my drug life. But there was no reaction. I had a boyfriend who provided me with illicit drugs and whatever I wanted. My mother knew him and did not even bother to tell me to break up with him. She did not even suggest it. Nor did she teach me about relationships with men; I mean, she did not explain private issues and what sexual relationships are about. She found out that I had sex with one of the guys in our neighbourhood, but she did not advise me in any way. One day, my cousin came to our home and my mother left me alone with him and went grocery shopping. My cousin raped me. When my mother came back and I told her, she just told me not to say a word to anyone. (Female participant, began using drugs at age nine)

The results show similar patterns for men who use substances; however, women are more sensitive to authoritative and directive parents who restrict and monitor them. Marjan, who was fifty-five with three children at the time of the study, was one of the most informative participants. She used heroin, was a drug dealer, and had been a sex worker for thirty years. In the previous five years of Marjan's life, she had lost everything she loved most, from her husband and children to boyfriends. Yet the worst part was her increasing propensity to use drugs. She described that she was abandoned by her family and was just one step away from death. According to Marjan:

My father was a military man and always expected everything at home to be organized, but he did not even hug me during his life. He managed and controlled every step we took in our life; he controlled my sisters and me. I really needed to be free and live for myself for just a second, but he did not let this happen to us. I always thought about getting married to set me free from my father's prison, so I decided to say yes to the first suggestion. However, my husband was addicted to heroin. My mother did not seem to see me at home, she just paid special attention to my older sister because she was so organized and clever, and she had a good performance at school. My mother never looked at me, she always punished me and my brothers for nothing. She locked us in a dark washroom for a full day. When I got married, she was so happy not to have to see me again. I felt lonely; I did not receive any support from my family. Even once I found out my husband used illicit drugs, my family decided to be passive in this situation as well. To set me free from an authoritative father, careless mother, and addict husband, I started to use heroin. (Female participant, began using drugs at age eighteen)

Some of the participants began using drugs to alleviate anxiety and chronic pain; drugs were offered to them to ease physical, mental, emotional, and psychological pain. Khadije lived with her parents, who were political activists during the Islamic Revolution. Her father set a schedule for his daughters to read the top one hundred historical books in the world. They had to write a summary of the books weekly. Her father always told her, "Khadije, you have to be a writer; you have to be a productive and important person in your country." However, she got married to a man who used substances, despite her father's objection. Her father told her, "Khadije, I'm sure you will fall into the drug trap if you get married to him." According to Khadije:

I always suffered from chronic pain during my period, and all the time my father-in-law and my husband, who were both addicted to heroin, suggested I should use drugs to relieve my pain. One time, when I could not find painkillers, I began to use heroin, and since then I have used the drug for 10 years. (Female participant, began using drugs at age eighteen)

Most participants had been witnesses to drug use among their loved ones and family members from a young age. They were indirectly taught that the best way to avoid or ignore the problems and issues around them was to be passive and use drugs. They felt powerless to change or even live their own lives. In fact, they used substances to cope with life challenges. Some of the participants declared that they did not simply want to try illicit drugs, but rather wanted to have a temporary respite.

> I feel like I have just been born—I do not know my emotions, I do not know how to manage and how to solve the problems in my life. I always put a cover on everything in my life by using drugs constantly. During the recovery process, I was faced with a huge range of emotions, from anger to love, which I had not allowed to surface before. I put a barrier on top of them, using drugs to mask them. I have started to know myself just now. Everything has become clear just now. I found out why my family left me, and why I lost my job and my best friends. I can analyze all those tragedies now. (Male participant, began using drugs at age twelve)

The most clear and transparent memory which was constantly repeated by the interviewees was the availability and common use of drugs in their families. They were not only eyewitnesses of substance consumption among their family members, but also they interacted with people who used substances and consequently were cajoled step by step to try drugs.

> I always smoked my father's cigarettes at night, and then one night I decided to try the opium in his pocket. It was relaxing; for hours, I did not feel any of the pains of my life. Every night, I would steal opium from his pocket until he left us, and then I abandoned my home to find drugs. My boyfriend was the next supplier of illicit drugs for me. (Female participant, began using drugs at age nine)

When parents or siblings use substances, it increases not only the availability of illicit drugs and the chance of using substances among the other members of the family, but also the possibility of abandonment. According to the interviews, out-of-home placements were the inevitable

36 Life on Drugs in Iran

result of substance use. Participants were left alone or with multiple caregivers, as most often their family members left them periodically without notification or discussion.

> We lived in the storage facility of a factory outside of the city; we literally lived in the desert. Around the factory there was no existence except us. We lived in poverty. My mother constantly told my father that we were hungry and needed food, but my father responded with violence and anger. Every month he left us for more than a week, and we had no idea how to survive in that scary place. The situation became worse when my mother decided to leave us. I cried and followed her and begged her to come back. I told her that I was scared, that I could not live without her, that I would die. But she did not care. She left us for weeks and then came back and the same story was repeated over and over for years. (Female participant, began using drugs at age nine)

> Besides all the fights between my parents throughout my childhood, being alone at home always troubled me. Different people took responsibility to take care of me, but I hated that situation. Even neighbors felt sorry about my situation and tried to give me some attention. My grandmother was another person who I had to live with for months. There was no papa, no mama. (Male participant, began using drugs at age fifteen)

Some participants did not learn about substance use or addiction until they were married. Then to make their marriage work and avoid conflict with the spouse's family, adapting their lifestyles was imperative:

> Although I had not seen drugs before in my life, my wife's family atmosphere and my foolish thoughts and ideas about being a good husband for her pushed me toward using drugs. I thought it might be a perfect strategy to present myself as a cool man in my wife's family. In addition, even if I did not want to use them, drugs were an inevitable part of all their parties. That was so tempting. (Male participant, began using drugs at age twenty-two)

Community was another source of addiction for participants of this study. Some found friends and neighbors as a well-positioned substitute for family members. It is not only family that acts as a trigger on the path towards addiction, but also the "isolated" communities and societies which play a significant role in compelling people toward addiction (Sampson and Lauritsen 1994). The negative effect of friendship groups can be reinforced in disadvantaged neighborhoods where illegal activities such as drug use and dealing may be common (Zahn 2007). According to Maghsodi et al. (2018), some participants encountered drugs through their social surroundings, although they did not claim that their family norms included such behaviors, nor were any of their family members a convicted felon.

> I had gone to one of my friends' homes where a brother was smoking drugs. It was there that I tested it and started smoking drugs. (Male participant, began using drugs at age sixteen)

Almost all participants took the same pathway to addiction; however, the time, process, and strategy of drug withdrawal might be different. From the first days of being trapped in addiction, the process of being excluded, stigmatized, and isolated began. The so-called war on drugs or anti-drug campaign in Iran is not only the state's strategy to combat drug-related offenders or people who use substances, but people with drug-free lifestyles use the same strategy to combat them through "poly-exclusion." According to Sanders (2014, 31), "the most stigmatizing social policy to date is the so-called war on drugs." In fact, before exclusion and stigmatization by the state is necessary, family can take charge of this mission—even those with a drug history. People who use substances in all institutions (e.g., family, education, religion, politics, economics) are considered human waste; drug addiction justifies, rationalizes, and legitimizes abusive behavior by the state. Family members and loved ones cannot tolerate the company of the one who uses substances, not because of dependence or physical deterioration, but because of the stigma and judgment of society toward addiction. The vehicle of the dehumanization of people who use drugs possesses an uncontrollable impetus when citizens with drug-free lifestyles subscribe to the views of the state.

My father only found a small packet of opium. Instead of talking to me or even asking about the owner, he called the police and I was arrested. He did not even want me to explain; I was trash to him, and he was ashamed of me. (Male participant, began using drugs at age twelve)

3

Prison

The Dehumanization Ceremony

New inmates follow an adjustment process at the time they enter custody. According to Goffman (1962), stripping self-esteem and degrading prisoners is considered an element of prison as a "total institution." Newcomers in the prison are subjected to informal social norms, which require an adaptation process. Although learning to live according to inmate social orders and codes sounds arduous (Vaughn and Sapp 1989), prisoners quickly understand that adaptation to prison subculture mitigates the pains of imprisonment (Sykes 1958).

People who use substances and are incarcerated in prison or compulsory camps have experienced a systematic "dehumanization" process. The dehumanization ceremony begins once people who use substances are arrested, whereupon they are locked up in temporary detention centers. Temporary detentions, according to the manager of the Kurdistan prison, are designed to protect potential offenders from the negative effects of incarceration. Then, people who use substances are processed to quarantine for almost a week and transferred to group cells. Some participants told of being whipped before being transferred to quarantine due to a positive drug test. Most of the cells in one of the prisons were thirteen meters in length with ten three-story beds; at the time of the study, almost all of the participants said that about sixty or even seventy prisoners were corralled in each cell. A few of the fortunate had beds, but the rest were confined to sleeping on the floor. The prisoners without available sleep arrangements are called *kaf khabha* (floor liers). At lunch time, just thirty of them could sit on the floor to eat their food, and the circumstances were

40   Life on Drugs in Iran

even more abhorrent for the units housing mothers and children. Incarcerated mothers and their children cannot use the second or third story of the beds in their cells since they incur significant risks for children. Some of the participants stated that there was not enough space even on the floor; they "slept" in the corridors during the first days of their incarceration. All the prisoners were stripped of their clothes and personal belongings, were subject to humiliation, and were subjugated to violation of their identities.

Ahmad was spending his recovery time in a voluntary camp. He had been processed through detoxification procedures more than eight times in both compulsory and voluntary institutions. For the sake of his family honor, he did not divulge the fact that he was whipped and incarcerated.

> I did not want to tell any of my relatives and friends that I got incarcerated. I did not even let my wife know about my incarceration because the length of incarceration was short, and I did not like that people would get to know about that. Once I got incarcerated, I got 35 lashes for being an addict. When I got released, I could not sleep on my back, so my family learned that I had been lashed and imprisoned." (Male participant, six months of incarceration)

Likewise, Ali was arrested on the street for consuming drugs and possessing 15 grams of heroin. Although for years he lived on the street as a *karton khab* (literally, "cardboard lier"), he was still disturbed by the cruel, inhumane, and degrading conditions in the prison.

> When I was incarcerated, I was ordered to wash the washrooms; I guess it was a tactic used by managers to ruin our pride and dignity. Prisoners are all made to wear Kurdi pants, which were called government pants. If you have any rings or hairstyle, you should give up your rings and you will be shaved. Also, you do not have any telephone coupons during the first week of incarceration. (Male participant, five years of incarceration)

The egregious circumstances experienced by inmates in drug-related prisons extend far beyond initial psychological pressure. In one facility, prisoners are not provided the most basic of necessities such as bed, food, or clothes.

> The situation there was awful. There was not enough food there, and I did not receive any toothbrush or underwear when I entered the prison. I washed my clothes and put them onto the heater to dry and then wore them again. I did not have any spare clothes. They did not give us a pillow, so I put my clothes under my head. (Female participant, three years of incarceration)

Rasoul was physically tortured via exposure to extreme cold and heat. At the time of incarceration, he was nineteen years old and raised in a religious family with no history of incarcerations or addictions.

> I was addicted to heroin, and I was sentenced to the death penalty for murder. I remember that I was in the police-enforced solitary confinement for 17 days. I was beaten so much there. They tortured us by moving us from extremely hot cells to extremely cold ones. Once I was moved to the prison, I was not given any appropriate clothes or even a towel. I was physically inspected. I was in quarantine for one week. That was torture because they humiliated us. (Male participant, six years of incarceration)

After the dehumanization ceremony, the process of prisonization begins. Six categories depict the lived experience of people who use substances in Iranian prions: (1) Unstable Pyramid, (2) Captive as a Society, (3) Battle Zone, (4) Hegemony of Drug-Related Networks, (5) Recriminalization and Re-drugization, and (6) Two Sides of the Same Coin.

Unstable Pyramid

Prison stability is challenged by several entities, including disobedient prisoners, informants, and transformed prisoners. In different circumstances, informal prison rules are disobeyed by inmates who are members of gangs not always willing to put their safety in jeopardy for the sake of other members and thereby subvert the cohesion of the gang. Although gang members are supposed to prove their loyalty by supporting other members in inter-gang violence, smuggling drugs, and snitching, on rare occasions they perceive a possibility that following their gang leader's orders would result in injury or death and consequently decide to retreat. Disobedient prisoners are not necessarily gang members; the desire to defeat high-status criminals to impose control is a routine maneuverer in prison life. However, such a tactic is occasionally successful. It disrupts the social order, subsequently shaking the foundation of prisoner solidarity. The most serious situation that undermines prison stability is the power struggle among gangs. There is always a dominant gang that presides over prison politics and competing gangs are constantly vying to overthrow them.

The other source of instability in prison is rooted in guards' fears of solidarity in prison society. By recruiting informants from among the prisoners for surveillance, guards undermine the loyalty and trust between prisoners. One might confuse the guards' natural interest in better knowing the prison society with their eagerness to discover drugs or related activities. While this may be a contributing factor, there are other motives—the goal is to reinforce a crime-oriented, not a treatment-oriented, atmosphere. In fact, continued attempts by prison administration to infiltrate groups and gangs with informants assures that solidarity and trust among the prison population is unattainable.

The final factor that undermines the stability of prison life is nested within intervention programs—in particular, NA. While the number of people in these programs is too few for the participants to be considered troublemakers, the crime-oriented policy of the prison system leaves no room for a treatment-oriented philosophy. NA members outside prisons passionately attempt to support the inmates through self-help programs, but guards, administrators, and prisoners themselves lack faith in these programs. Some inmates do join these programs, where their involvement and practice of NA principles represent defiance to gang legitimacy. NA members may leave the gang and protest established orders and rules. Ultimately, NA participants are not true opponents of gangs or high-status criminals; they do not seek power or status, but rather seek to promote rules and codes based on NA principles. This goal can be achieved with intense resistance and opposition.

The Dehumanization Ceremony 43

In fact, neither dominant statuses nor hierarchy criteria are fixed in prison. Social orders follow the negotiations of social construction, and social orders and norms are transformed when those in charge are changed. Living in a precarious shifting zone, where no one presides for long, forces inmates to deal with continuous difficulties associated with adjusting to new social codes after the dominant group has changed. Wrestling with multiple identities is not only an issue once inmates arrive in prison; rather, it is a continuing quandary.

> We have to admit that the dominant group in the prison was not stable. Likewise, in society, everything is updated every day. The criminal skills and drugs are being changed over time. When I was incarcerated, we did not know about methamphetamine, but during recent years, young people from the wealthy regions of the city who are familiar with new drugs and new forms of crimes are the dominant group in the prison. Forms of managing the prison, even fighting, languages, everything, are being changed gradually. Sometimes, a group of prisoners will set up a fight with the dominant group in the prison, and if they win, they take their position, then all the prisoners will be under their wing. What I mean is that managing is not in the hands of one group always; it has been changing as time passes. (Male participant, nine years of incarceration)

Under these circumstances, where social orders serve as the most unstable and unattainable of concepts, the conflict between identities is not a matter of conflict between prisoners' former and institutional identities. It is a clash between one's previous and imminent identity; inmates constantly chase novel social orders. A dominant group should attain the full cooperation of other prisoners by establishing a new, informal code of conduct for effective prison societal management. The challenge of adjusting to these new orders exposes inmates to multiple identities. Although criminologists believe the former identity of inmates gradually decays during incarceration, my findings establish that those who use substances suffer from the coexistence of multiple identities. The previous identities do not decay nor are they stripped; they fade, but still exist.

44 Life on Drugs in Iran

> Most of us do not know how to deal with the different situation in prison. You know why, because, if you are not familiar with different rules and norms, which obviously are not stable, you might accidently break one of them and then God help you. I, sometimes, don't know who I am. I must adjust to different and stupid rules. Who I was before being incarcerated is still with me. Sometimes I forget it, but it's still there. (Male participant, five years of incarceration)

Inmates struggle with unstable or even contradictory circumstances. First and foremost, prisoners are exposed to the inner conflict between the established orders of the outside and inside worlds; this transpires even if they were previously engaged in a criminal subculture before incarceration. These circumstances can be even more frustrating for prisoners who use substances and are not involved with the criminal lifestyle. In circumstances where a prisoner with no former criminal record and no regular contacts with criminals is incarcerated for heroin possession in excess of thirty grams, they are sentenced to death, forced to live in prison as their final home, and forced to adopt multiple identities.

> If you are just one who uses substances, you are nothing in the prison. You must be a criminal and drug dealer to change others' minds toward you. Once I was imprisoned, I was like trash; nobody communicated with me. I did not even know how to talk and with whom to talk. I did not know how to manage my life among those criminals. I was scared. I did not belong to this place. I was just one who used substances and carried 30 grams of heroin for my own usage. I was shocked once I heard about the sexual relationships between women in the prison. I just could not believe how it might be possible. I heard about the drug trafficking in the prison, but I did not see it. I slept in the corridors. I did not see anything. I was not allowed to see anything. They assaulted each other constantly. The words were so strange to me. It took months and months for me to get used to this situation. I tried to put aside everything that I knew and started from scratch. (Female participant, two years of incarceration)

Most incarcerated with opioid addiction were involved in unpremeditated violent acts (e.g., murder) while high on drugs. Many of these

The Dehumanization Ceremony   45

individuals did not have regular contact with criminals and were not familiar with the code of behavior before their imprisonment.

It is true that I am a murderer, but I did not have constant communication with criminals. I was addicted to heroin and when I was high, I killed my friend in a fight. I entered the prison and did not know what to do. I was a murderer and all the prisoners expected me to act as a murderer, but I did not. I was not a murderer. I did not know how murderers act or behave. My personality was torn apart. I lost myself. Every second in the prison I reminded myself that you are in the prison and must act as a murderer. You are not outside. These struggles still follow me, even now after 9 years. (Male participant, nine years of incarceration)

Financial issues are one of the significant reasons identified for engaging in drug trafficking, especially among incarcerated women. These women are the principal breadwinners of the family and in many cases have been abandoned by husbands who use substances. The welfare of their children and saving them from misery were derived to be the sole motives to be involved in drug smuggling.

I was arrested for delivering one kilogram of heroin from Bandar Abbas to Isfahan to afford to live. I have seven children whose lives are in my hands. I was the breadwinner of my home, as my husband was an addict, and he abandoned us three years ago. I was addicted to opium myself, but it was pervasive and usual in our tribe that people use opium. I did not know anything about crimes and criminals. One day I decided to do something for my children to make them happy, because I could not afford even their food. My sister had five children and her husband was also addicted. She and I decided to transfer drugs to another city, and in return, we were promised that we would earn 500,000 toman ($70 USD in 2017). That was so much money for us. We did it, but we got arrested in Isfahan. I cannot forget the day my sister and I got imprisoned in the central prison of Isfahan. We did not know anything, I mean anything, about the life in the prison. We were scared to the extent that when we entered the prison, we did not even go to the yard for one month. My sister, she's older than me, she told the guards that we didn't know how to survive in this place and asked them to help us. As time passed, every day we changed. We each became another person. We still have difficulties getting used to the prison life because it is completely new in our lives. I did not know how to find drugs in the prison, I did not even know that you could find it in the prison easier than outside. I was a mother, and I had seven children. How could I deal with criminals every second? Those challenges made me crazy. The day the judge told us you are sentenced to the death penalty, we fell on the floor. We are on death row now after five years of living in prison and I barely see my children. I have to say that it is not our place. It is not. (Female participant, nine years of incarceration)

Prisoners struggle simultaneously with unstable and contradictory circumstances, experiencing conflict between their prior and continuously evolving new identities. Meanwhile, the contradictory criteria of the prevailing hierarchy contribute to strengthening these conflicting identities. Brutally violent criminals who are financially independent, manage the cells, and possess sufficient authority to manage drug networks are revered. Conversely, inmates who are innocent, spiritually attuned, seniors, *loti* (honorable and high-minded), and *rish sefid* (mediators) are subject to approbation as well. As a result, these cumulative contradictions compel prisoners to live in a state of limbo in which they must adjust accordingly. Although the status of prisoners is determined by their criminal history, wealth, spiritual identity, social capital, sexuality, loyalty, and control over drug networks, the focus calibrated here is on the impact of drugs on the prisoners' status.

It is well documented that drug dealers in prison have cultivated considerable respect and status (Crewe 2005, 2006). Crewe (2005) and Mjåland (2014, 2016) attribute this enhanced respect and status to the completion of high-risk activities, such as inmates risking their lives smuggling drugs into prison. However, in the current study, the respect and admiration these individuals receive is completely based on the fact that they are providing a basic need (i.e., drugs). However, not all inmates are allowed to smuggle drugs into prison, and another basis for power, such as violent criminal records or ties with high-status criminals, is required. Otherwise, drug possession would not be commensurate for access to higher degrees of power, status, or respect.

> You have to fit into a certain position for importing drugs into the prison; in other words, these clothes (drugs) have to fit on your body. Someone who has drugs or delivers drugs to the prison should have a special personality or characteristics. I mean, he must be someone who others can count on, he must be a violent criminal such as a murderer, and he must be tough and serious. Otherwise, he must have connections with powerful criminals within the prison. I was a murderer, and I did not have a strong body, but the way that I behaved with others meant that nobody dared to bully me. I would say "hi" to others reluctantly. Others told themselves that "he is a murderer—how do I dare to tell him something inappropriate?" I was a person who could deliver drugs. Also, I had strong connections with *tighdarha* (violent criminals). (Male participant, ten years of incarceration)

Prisoner status and drugs are different spokes of the same wheel; the former is changed by transferring the latter. The exclusive right to smuggle drugs in custody is in the hands of leaders (almost all of whom are drug traffickers and murderers), who are treated with unfathomable esteem. This exclusive power and control are exercised over drugs and inmates in custody.

> I was incarcerated for more than 25 years. I transported drugs from Afghanistan to northern Iran while I was in the prison. Nobody dared to transfer drugs into this specific region of Iran. It was my territory. Yes, I was in prison, but I had constant control over drug trafficking in my city. I delivered drugs to the prison every time I was on leave, and, I had four fellows who smuggled drugs. There was not anybody in the prison whom I was supposed to respect, even the correctional officers; the officers, even those guys, should respect me. You know what? They did know how powerful I was. All the prisoners asked for drugs from me and if they themselves wanted to deliver drugs to the prison, they first asked me. (Male participant, thirty years of incarceration)

48 Life on Drugs in Iran

> We not only had control over drugs in the prison, but also we governed the prison through drugs. We governed the whole prison system through drugs. We were eight prisoners who had possession over all the drugs in the prison. Every two weeks, one of us went on leave and brought back drugs to the prison. (Male participant, seven years of incarceration)

Prisoners exploit the sympathy of correctional officers; it is avowed that the officers express compassion to murderers on death row. As such, their wards, in contrast to others, do not receive regular inspections, making them one of the most secure locations to conceal drugs. Most often, leaders and high-status criminals do not jeopardize their lives by delivering drugs into the prison or between units within the prison. Instead, they recruit *anbari* (storage people or mules) to transport the drugs inside their body cavities. Cooperation with guards can facilitate the process of smuggling drugs into and within the prison.

> Most of them are untraceable, and you do not know by whom or when the drugs will be delivered to the prison. (Male participant, five years of incarceration, NA representative in the prison)

Captive as a Society

Deprivation is a shared characteristic of prisons worldwide, yet this condition does not apply to leaders' lives inside the prison. I found that leaders, especially drug traffickers, have built a palace equipped with facilities and private spaces at the heart of the prison which gives rise to their appellations as the "kings of prison."

> He was so powerful in prison no one could beat him. He literally has a *kakh* (palace) in prison. Whatever you want you can find it there, just name it. Of course, it was not like your life outside the prison, yet something not like a prison life. He was king. He has money, he bought privacy and luxury life inside. (Male participant, ten years of incarceration)

Although transparency and exposure in prison limits inmate privacy and inmates are even strongly advised to be open about their crimes,

The Dehumanization Ceremony   49

prisoners are advised not to peer into other's cells or beds. This unwritten rule applies on most occasions for those in custody but serves as an absolute requirement for high-status criminals and those related to the leaders, and those who consume drugs or are involved in sexual activities. Some cells have private areas called *dakhme* (cellar) between the beds that are dedicated to drug usage.

> We were consuming drugs in our *dakhme*, then we realized SB was checking on us. He was just arrested and was trying to find drugs. He did not know that what he was doing was parallel with death. (Male participant, six years of incarceration)

> Nobody dares to even take a sneaky look into the rooms of high-status criminals. You have to sign your death certificate if they are using drugs in [their] *dakhme* and then notice your curiosity. They are high and don't see anything. You will be dead. Newcomers who are not familiar with the rules sometimes do silly acts. I remember one of them ran into a sexual scene and he was shocked and did not know the rules, thus, he was beaten so bad just because he stared at them. Then he took his lesson to not look at anywhere but your feet. (Male participant, four years of incarceration)

The constant and inevitable internal struggle experienced by prisoners and the precondition of adding physical survival to their basic needs is vital in the prison system. The complicated and obfuscated coexistence of privacy and transparency result in contradictory social actions, which are barriers to the emergence of unit-based identities in prison. The accumulation of criminal history and a degree of economic and social capital is a precondition for deserved privacy in a highly transparent institution. A wealthy, professional drug trafficker in custody is guaranteed tremendous financial opportunities through multiple channels, including prisoners and correctional officers. There are only one or two "kings" in each prison with exclusive authority within the prison territory, and in the drug community within the broader society. The incarceration of wealthy professional drug dealers serves to expand their social networks from society to the penal system which ultimately affords exclusive control over the price and demand for drugs, and provides financial incentives for correctional officers. According to one participant with approximately thirty years of incarceration experience across Iran and years of criminal history as a leading drug trafficker from Afghanistan to Northern Iran:

> I did not eat regular food in the prison; I ordered food and some of my friends brought my orders to the prison for me. The bars of my cell were always closed and were covered with a curtain. That was not usual in the prison. Nobody was allowed to cover their door with a curtain; they could not even cover their own beds with anything. Everything had to be as transparent as possible. Everybody is a witness to all your activities. However, that did not apply to prisoners like me. I remember one time when I got incarcerated, the correctional officers knew me well. I was notified that they wanted to come to arrest me, so I did not escape. I stayed in my house in the jungle and waited for them. When they came, I told them that I had to bring my private belongings into the prison. I was incarcerated in solitary confinement for one month with all my private belongings. They all knew me; whenever I was incarcerated, they knew that a large amount of drugs would be transferred to the prison without a doubt. I ignored the prison's rules, but I made friends with the guards. Although they knew that by incarcerating me nothing was going to happen in the society, they still incarcerated me. Some of them were very cooperative with me when it came to delivering drugs.

Prison leaders recruit young low-status inmates as "minions" (*noche*) to spy on other gangs and sections, and to provide high-profile information about inmates and correctional officers. The subculture of *noche parvari* (*noche* refers to a novice young man as a petty servant) is a common phenomenon in prison. The *noche* have a subordinate position; however, in exchange for revealing sensitive information, leaders provide them with luxuries from the best quality drugs to food and bedding, which immediately improves their lives compared to their peers. Therefore, vulnerable and low-status criminals are shielded from victimization under the protection of the leader. The nature of reciprocity, that forms relationships between the kings and their subordinates, is based on the exchange of information and materials which leads to the creation of the *noche* status.

The existence of leaders in prison is determined by not only their occupation, wealth, and an exclusive authority over drug dealing, but also by the accuracy of information delivered by the *noche*.

Despite the unwritten rules in the underworld requiring that one does not disclose confidential information or act as an informant, tattling for the kings builds credit with them quickly, in stark contrast with delivering information to correctional officers. Prisoners know who the *noche* are, and that they are protected by the most powerful leader in the prison.

> Prisoners, such as myself, who are wealthy and take charge of drug trafficking in the prison have 7 or 8 *noche* around us. I had *noche* outside of the prison as well. In the prison, they updated me with fresh news about events that had happened in the prison. They notified me of whatever they had seen or heard that might affect my position in the prison. I did not give them money. I had a handkerchief that was soaked with heroin. I brought that into the prison; that handkerchief was drenched with a half kilogram of heroin. In return for protecting my powerful status in the prison by snitching and flattering, I gave them a small part of my handkerchief. I provided them with good-quality food and a bed in the prison and even helped them outside of the prison when they got released. (Male participant, thirty years of incarceration)

The only prisoners who are not stigmatized and whose status is not degraded and affected by homosexual activities are the kings. Likewise, there are reciprocal relationships between the king (*arbab*) and the servant (*noche*), where the subordinate sexual partners support the emotional and sexual needs of their overseers and receive food, drugs, and a bed in exchange. The subordinate sexual partners, almost all of whom have a low status in the penal world, tolerate all the weight of stigma in prison. Meanwhile, the homosexual activities of kings are not considered shameful or dishonorable; rather they are perceived as a sign of power. High-status criminals in women's prisons have sexual partners as well, and this is not stigmatized, nor is it a source of shame. Those who are severely monitored or stigmatized are low-status prisoners. The stigma of homosexuality can affect all manner of prisoners except for high-status, violent criminals who constantly govern the prison schedule.

52 Life on Drugs in Iran

> Some of the leaders in prison, who have always been violent criminals, have sexual partners, but no one would dare to report any of their homosexual activities in prison. They are violent criminals with long-term experiences in prison. They are proud of having sexual partners. (Female participant, two years of incarceration)

Not all homosexual activities in the penal world involve physical contact. On some occasions, high-status prisoners do not have any physical contact with their sexual partners; they desire their companionship for comfort. These individuals are called *rokh baz* (someone who enjoys a beautiful face) or *mashami* (someone who enjoys a beautiful scent)

> When the cell's boss takes a beautiful prisoner under his wing, it means that he belongs to him. Most of them are *rokh baz*, who do not touch their partners; it just feels sexy to communicate with these beautiful guys. When they cannot have intercourse, they use their eyes. Just by looking and smelling they gain sexual satisfaction. (Male participant, four years of incarceration)

> He just gave me a bed and as much as food as I wanted. He gave me the bed closest to himself. He hired someone to wash my clothes. I did not do anything. He enjoyed my company. He did not let me do anything. I did not know what he wanted. Once I came to the prison, he chose me and told me that I had to stay by his side. (Male participant, seven months of incarceration)

Battle Zone

Virtually all of the violence perpetrated in prison revolves around three factors: drugs, sex, and safety. Since drugs play a crucial role in prisoners' survival behind bars, even the smallest disorganization in the system of distribution is considered intolerable. The systematic distribution of methadone by the health department plays a pivotal role in deescalating any possible risk of violence resulting from prisoners suffering withdrawal. Methadone is the most pervasive form of medication-assisted treatment in the Iranian penal system. Methadone treatment consists of a daily dose prescription and costs about $5 USD per person per month in 2017. Methadone therapy was considered a cost-effective and practical treatment for heroin addiction; however, most inmates stated that they use methadone in prison while still consuming other available drugs. The official policy for distributing methadone in custody targets two goals: treating addiction and decreasing violence. By paying approximately $5 USD per month, inmates were provided with a certain amount of methadone, which was administered by a physician every morning and dosed proportionately in accordance with the prisoner's drug use history. However, neither goal behind the methadone maintenance treatment is achieved. In fact, polydrug use and pervasive, drug-related violence in the prison system demonstrates the inept disorganization of treatment programs that are repeatedly defeated by the securitization policy.

Most fights in prison happen because of drugs; for the 3 months that I was incarcerated in prison, I fought around 40 times over drugs. I remember one day when drugs were prohibited in the prison, prisoners set up a protest to fight and beat guards, forcing them to make drugs available. Drugs are like oxygen for us in the prison. Any slight move against drug use will face an extreme reaction from the prisoners. Nobody in the cell dares to protest against other inmates using drugs in the cell, or they will be beaten so hard. (Male participant, ten years of incarceration)

I was in the *Kanon* (a separate section in prison for youth) for 6 months. When I turned 18 years old, I was moved to the central prison. One of the biggest and most violent rebellions I had ever seen in the prison happened in the *Kanon*. The rebellion started from a small fight between two friends because of drugs, and suddenly about 100 prisoners started to fight. The chaos was so bad that the guards ran away. The prisoners exploded all the fire extinguishers. At last, at midnight, two buses full of guards with tear gas (lachrymators) invaded the prison. Beforehand, the ward of the prison with the Quran in his hand came to the prison and told us "I swear on the Quran I will not do anything if you let me in." We let him in, and he just moved the main perpetrators of the disaster, and we did not see them again. (Male participant, seven years of incarceration)

54 Life on Drugs in Iran

According to Article 42 of the Anti-Narcotic Law of Iran, "the Judicature power is permitted to maintain some of the drug-related convicts in special camps (with tight or normal conditions) rather than prisons. The government has a duty to provide necessary funds, facilities and regulations for managing such camps in a period of one year." In keeping with this strategy, compulsory labor camps were established exclusively for drug-related criminals. According to the interlocutors, labor camps are the most disorderly and chaotic institutions for people who use substances; almost all inmates in the labor camps continually consume drugs. Violence was widespread, and some prisoners declared that "it [was] inevitable." In the labor camps, inmates were surrounding by people who actively use substances and drug traffickers and thereby render a disparate array of drugs to be made available and affordable (i.e., cheaper than in any other type of prison) which led to a preponderance of drug overdose deaths. These camps were nothing more than a locked space for those who use substances and dealers in a chaotic world. Although inmates in the labor camps were employed, the minimum wage was $7 USD monthly, which caused most inmates to refuse to work. Those who agreed to work in prison factories were granted some privileges, including extra phone minutes and in-person visits with family. In addition to the respective formal advantages, those who chose to work in labor camp factories gradually created a black market by stealing the factory products.

> The drug-related units in the prison were the most dangerous and unsafe parts of the prison. To punish prisoners in other sections, especially murderers, they would move them to the drug section. There were continued fights among prisoners who could not be controlled at all. Even with methadone being distributed every day, there are several prisoners who need other drugs as well. Some of them did not have money, and they would do anything to get drugs. If one group of prisoners found out about the existence of drugs in another cell, they would fight to take their drugs. (Male participant, three years of incarceration)

> I was in a camp which was established for drug-related offenders. Actually, I wanted to escape from that prison because it was unbearable. I

The Dehumanization Ceremony   55

went to sleep one night, and in the morning, my cellmate next to me had passed away; he had overdosed. It was difficult to see someone to pass away next to you because of drugs. There were a wide variety of drugs in that prison, and the price was not as high as in other prisons. For example, if drugs were 100,000 toman[1] in camp, they cost 300,000[2] toman in other prisons. The opportunity for using drugs in camp was more than in prison. Although it was a fact that all kinds of offenders, from murderers to drug traffickers, were incarcerated in the prison, and they had to deal with violent criminals. In the camp, several people died because of drugs. Therefore, there was no difference between these two prisons. Most of the prisoners in the camp would even prefer to be in prison. (Male participant, five years of incarceration)

While male prisoners pervasively witnessed or were involved in physical violence and fighting in custody, this is not the case in female prisons. While not the potential victim of a violent act in prison, female prisoners preferred to remain silent and obedient as long as possible to avoid jeopardizing their lives. However, this does not mean there were no traces of violence in women's sections; verbal violence is more common among incarcerated women.

I do not want to say that we did not fight or beat each other, but most often we were just insulting and making up rumors about each other. (Female participant, five years of incarceration)

There were some rumors that some prisoners knifed someone to death, but we did not see or experience anything ourselves. We feared those prisoners, so we did everything that they wanted. We avoided any kind of fighting. (Female participant, three years of incarceration)

It is worth noting that violence is also a pervasive phenomenon in compulsory camps, which are designed and organized to house people

1. $2 USD
2. $7 USD

56   Life on Drugs in Iran

who use substances and to coerce abstinence from drugs. Violence is seen as the ideal approach to maintain control over those who use substances in camps, as many are not prepared to quit. In fact, most have never been involved in criminal activities or been in possession of drugs at the time of their arrest. Those who are suspected of being involved in drug activities based on their appearance or behavior were arrested by anti-narcotic police officers in the name of the "purification plan" (*tarh-e paksazi*). In these circumstances, there is no plan for suspects, but this does not deter the police from interrogation on the grounds of drug suspicion. As one female participant with several experiences in compulsory camps and prisons stated:

> From the beginning to the end of the process, we are victims of severe violence beyond your imagination. Police enforcers, in front of everybody on the street, forced us to get into their car. They did not even pay attention to my four-year-old girl. The last time I was arrested on the street, I was with her. Can you imagine that they did not even look at my child? She cried and shouted in the street until one of my friends in the night drop-in center saw us and came to pick her up from the street. If you show resistance to getting in the car, you will be beaten hard and assaulted. When they transferred us to the camp, we had to wait in a line for a drug test, and if it was positive, the misery began. There is no soft language over there. You must listen to the personnel, or you will be beaten. The answer to even slightly bad behavior is violence. You know why? Because none of the addicts there want to quit drugs. They break glass and throw everything. The personnel are forced to calm them down by threatening them or beating them.

Hegemony of Drug-Related Networks

Although the pain of imprisonment and pre-incarceration pathways of inmates' lives play a pivotal role in the emergence of an inmate code and informal social order in the penal system, the subculture of prisons in Iran is affected to a great extent by the hegemony of the drug network. Correctional officers have declared that almost all inmates with a severe addiction maintain drug habits in prison which encourages others (i.e.,

The Dehumanization Ceremony   57

with drug-free lifestyle) to follow suit as a strategic plan to gain acceptance into the prison community (i.e., to be eligible to socialize with other inmates at their gatherings) or to handle emotional distress. Some inmates habitually used drugs before their incarceration to cope with depression and anxiety as a form of self-medication (Mjåland 2016) and necessarily, incarceration intensifies substance use disorder. The extent of drug use in prison depends on prison circumstances (e.g., availability and prevalence). There is a wealth of literature on the prevalence and availability of drugs in prisons (e.g., Emcdda 2012; Friestad and Hansen 2005; Boys et al. 2000; Stover and Weilandt 2007; Strang et al. 2006; Bullock 2003; Plugge et al. 2009; Hucklesby and Wilkinson 2001; Edgar and O'Donnell 1998). Interviews with people who use substances, consultants, and people in recovery revealed a crucial impact of drugs on the prison community.

> There were unwritten rules in the prison, and whether you like it or not, whether it is your preference or not, you have to accept and practice them. Drug use was a pervasive phenomenon in prison, and if you did not use drugs, you would undoubtedly be excluded. Imagine that from 10,000 prisoners, 9,900 prisoners used drugs. I was in a cell with 12 cellmates, all of whom were addicts, and I had to use drugs to be a part of them. I had to live a life there for however many years; it was my home. (Male participant, ten years of incarceration)

> When I entered the central prison, I was just 18 years old. I had to smoke something in the prison, because it was so inappropriate not to smoke. Because I was a murderer, I had committed a violent crime, and everybody respected me. If I did not smoke drugs in the prison, other prisoners would call me a "pasteurized murderer" (a murderer who was too naïve and unprofessional to commit a murder). I did everything that was possible in the prison because of the atmosphere. Yes, I started to use drugs. (Male participant, six years of incarceration)

When drugs are imported into the penal system, the distribution process, which involves complex connections and logistics, is initiated. The professional and powerful drug traffickers recruit inmates to sell and deliver drugs in different units. As noted earlier, illicit drugs in Iranian prisons are ten times more expensive than their usual price in the outside world, which prompts their epithet among prisoners as "prison gold." A lack of cash in prison is not an impediment to the drug trade, as transactions occur between both parties (buyer and seller) by the exchange of the most in-demand materials, such as phone cards, food and clothes. On some occasions, prisoners requested funds from their associates outside to be transferred to a specific account provided by the dealers. However, if prisoners cannot finance their consumption by exchanging valuable materials or taking on debt from the outside world, they inevitably fall into two categories: (1) stealing from and bullying other prisoners, or (2) agreeing to be a servant or a passive sexual partner of high-status prisoners. In both cases, the perceptible proclivity towards degradation of one's social status and honor is inordinate. One might think that the wheels of the drug trade and enterprise in the penal system are turned merely through money, and this is partially true as exploiting the profitable drug business was brought up by prisoners constantly. However, this is only one side of the coin—the resulting dependency and power take various forms.

People who use substances are already powerless and subordinate in the correctional system. They become increasingly dependent upon fellow inmates who are providers as the only hope to meet a crucial need (i.e., drugs). This dependency on drugs provides high-status drug traffickers with absolute control over an obedient crew to expand their power and influence over inmates and thereby garner greater reverence. As Crewe (2005, 470) states, "power and respect are frequently conflated." All inmates in the penal system, whether those who use substances or drug-free inmates, are thoroughly immersed in the drug market. As interviewees repeatedly testified, ninety percent of inmates in each cell use substances; thus, drug-free prisoners are indirectly exposed to the high-status dealers' influence throughout the prison and are also harassed by drug-using cellmates to whom they are indebted.

Drugs are the most profitable business in prison, which increases opportunities to exercise power in the prison system; this trade is exploited by high-status drug dealers and correctional officers. Therefore, it is indisputable that the drug business in the penal world is a pillar of power and perhaps the only means for prisoners to control their lives. They are

The Dehumanization Ceremony   59

provided with ample opportunities to explore their desires for using or selling drugs which in turn assists those in power (i.e., prison managers) to recognize, categorize, identify, and control prisoners. The social behaviors within the prisoners' circle of substance use and their functionality largely rest on drugs. Therefore, instead of managing prisoners by recruiting well-educated correctional officers and providing adequate rehabilitation and treatment programs, drugs themselves are governing prisons. Managing and monitoring inmates with minimum rehabilitation and training programs would not be feasible without the sedation of drugs, which is the most cost-effective and profitable strategy. As a result of this power being unceasingly exploited by high-status drug traffickers, continual negotiation and trade occurs between the respective drug traffickers and correctional officers to enhance the efficiency, manageability, and accessibility of this control mechanism.

> All guards know who delivers drugs to the prison; this is exactly what they want. (Male participant, five years of incarceration)

> All of the prisoners in our cell, about 80 people, used heroin. Even the wardens were witnessing our drug consumption in the yard and did not care at all. (Male participant, nine years of incarceration)

Methadone was also considered a control mechanism in prison and was constantly distributed to prisoners via the prison medical center. Virtually all inmates considered methadone as another addictive drug.

> If we did not use methadone in prison, there was a fight every day. Methadone was distributed to calm down prisoners. (Male participant, five years of incarceration)

> Methadone was distributed in prison at a specific time of day. Methadone was distributed among prisoners for three reasons: (1) To medicate people who use drugs, (2) To make them calm, and (3) To decrease the risk of shared injections and HIV. Not only do they use methadone but also all other kinds of drugs. (Male participant, nine years of incarceration)

60   Life on Drugs in Iran

It is true that a percentage of all cases of violence is directly driven by drugs; however, managing drug networks reduces violence overall. Illegal drugs are levers by which chaos and protests are handled along with prisoners' bodies and minds. Maintaining a steady stream of drugs into prisons indirectly institutes a predictable pattern of behavior. Inmates become passive objects in prison, as they were in society before their incarceration. Their dependency on drugs continues in custody and may worsen due to lack of communication with their families. Consequently, drugs become their last haven.

> It was impossible to cut the drugs from the prison, and no matter what section of the prison you were in you could find syringes. In our section, there were 700 prisoners who were all heroin addicts. If they did not have heroin, they turned into monsters. So, how could guards control them? Just by controlling the transfer of drugs into prison. (Male participant, ten years of incarceration)

> Five years ago, a prison's warden decided to abandon drugs in the prison; there were a lot of protests against this decision and a lot of people were killed. Then, they did not ever abandon drugs. They found out that prisoners are more manageable by using drugs than without them. (Male participant, seven years of incarceration)

Corrupt officers play a significant role in maintaining the drug system in the heart of the penal world; their cooperation makes its existence possible. Besides their financial interest[3] and attempts to minimize the risk of protests and to manage the prison society overall, there is also a lack of belief in the functionality of prison facilities; this ranges from treatment to training and consulting services for death row inmates. For prisoners on death row, abandonment by their most cherished is a cause for alliance.

> It felt so bad to admit the fact that all prisons' managers tend to distribute drugs in the prison. They themselves kept some doors open

---

3. To be explained in detail in the "Two Sides of the Same Coin" section.

to allow drug transferring to the prison. The most important reason was that, for example, in our section, there were about 400 prisoners without any sign of hope in their faces; their family members were not there to support them emotionally. Most of them did not have any visits from their family. Along with that, the prisoners, cell mates, and guards do not have that much capacity to support each other. Thus, the only thing to keep them calm was drugs. (Male participant, six years of incarceration)

For high-status drug traffickers, life in outside society and within the prison walls is similar. However, in terms of economic gain, selling drugs in prison is the far more profitable endeavor. The penal system functions as the most economically secure region with the greatest profits for dealers. By incarcerating people who use drugs, conditions for the most profitable business are created. A former prisoner declared:

The best-quality drugs with the highest price have been transferred to the prison, just to control prisoners. (Male participant, five years of incarceration)

In prison, the economics of the drug business is encapsulated by one simple rule: the more people who use substances imprisoned, the more profit obtained. Having exclusive and ultimate power over trading drugs at the highest price in a restricted area is more feasible and risk-free than in the outside world. There are no competitors to affect the price or offer affordable alternatives; the monopoly of the drug business lies in the hands of the leaders who gain the most profit. It is also cost-effective in terms of logistics; drugs can be in the hands of the buyer in less than five minutes.

You can buy drugs in the prison quicker and easier than outside; if it takes one hour to buy drugs outside, it takes just one minute to buy and use drugs inside the prison. (Male participant, nine years of incarceration)

If there was no bread in the prison, you could just use hashish instead. (Male participant, seven years of incarceration)

62   Life on Drugs in Iran

Property and strip searching (i.e., physically examining naked prisoners) occurs regularly, and especially to those who use substances. When units are inspected, drug-free inmates are pressured to conceal cellmates' drugs since they are not suspected by officers. A wide range of coercion strategies, from offering a pack of cigarettes to a telephone card, are used as collateral. There are three main routes of smuggling drugs into the prison: prisoners (i.e., via travel in and out of prison by leave or furlough), corrupt officers, and visiting family members. Some prisoners smuggle drugs into the prison for their personal consumption; in some cases, however, a group of prisoners is recruited by high-status criminals to smuggle drugs for the boss. On occasion, criminals will expose themselves intentionally so they can be imprisoned and subsequently sell drugs in prison at a premium. Drug smuggling in prison is a lucrative business platform for some drug dealers, which serves as a more profitable endeavor than dealing outside the confines of the prison.

> Kurdish prisoners are well known for delivering drugs by storing them in their body. They made fake scenes to get arrested and sell drugs and then get released. They come with just 50 grams of opium and get released with a large box of money. (Male participant, four years of incarceration)

Family visits were another potential channel used to smuggle drugs. Drugs were passed from family members, especially spouses and parents, to inmates during in-person visits when expressing physical affection (i.e., hugs or kisses), or in boxes of food or clothes. Some prisoners stash drugs under the visiting room carpet for another inmate to retrieve during cleaning duties and store in their body before returning to their cell. The riskiest pathway for transferring drugs into the prison is through family members in the visiting room, as nearly all these family members lack experience with the criminal lifestyle, and a naïve decision can easily foil the plan. The main intention of drug smuggling through the family route is not for personal consumption; rather, it is a means to financially support the inmates and their family through the lucrative prison drug network.

The Dehumanization Ceremony 63

However, this was not the only purpose. According to Islamic law, the punishment for deliberate homicide is the death penalty (*qisas*) or the payment of blood money (*diyat*).[4] Therefore, for those inmates who are sentenced to death but the victim's relatives are reluctant to insist on *qisas*, the best way to accrue adequate finances for blood money is to participate in the drug trade in prison. Given the premium price on drugs in prison, families often deliver them to inmates.

> My mother smuggled drugs to prison to help me financially. I wanted to sell the drugs to earn money and afford my life in prison and to pay some portion of my debts and afford the payment of blood money. I stored them in my body where it couldn't be searched. After that, every time my mother brought me drugs. But that was so risky, because sometimes we are strip searched, and the officers may find that. (Female participant, seven years of incarceration)

Recriminalization and Re-drugization

While the dominant discourse of correctional facilities is focused on distributing punishment rather than rehabilitation and treatment, the efforts of prisoners are dedicated to surviving the prison's circumstances. Their most popular form of entertainment includes bragging about their criminal skills and escapades while socializing and using drugs. The recriminalization process compensates for the lack of a rehabilitation program.

> Prison is the best educational workshop ever. All prisoners talked about their criminal activities and others were all ears to learn. I got put in prison because of a car robbery, and I got released with enough

---

4. "In cases of deliberate homicide, *diyat* is due only when the nearest relatives of the victim do not insist on *qisas* . . . Whenever the relatives insist upon the payment of *diyat*, it is to be in the value of one hundred camels . . . Although *diyat* is originally fixed in terms of camels, it is almost universally admitted that it can be paid by an equivalent amount of money, either gold or silver, cows, sheep or garments" (Pervin 2016, 145).

knowledge about housebreaking. (Male participant, three years of incarceration)

Long-term prisoners become far more adept in committing crimes than their counterparts residing outside the prison. The logistics associated with drug trafficking are meticulously refined; they smuggle drugs more efficiently in terms of time management, profit, and quantities than before their arrest. In other words, since illicit drugs are consumed and transferred under the careful surveillance of correctional officers, prisoners learn to achieve the same result with less effort after their release. Although the prison drug trade is facilitated through guards' cooperation, these activities occur under security surveillance. As such, inmates are equipped with enhanced criminal skills and become proficient in practicing these skills in the most secure location possible (i.e., prison). Thus, drug trafficking outside prison without the constant surveillance of officers and guards is far less complicated.

Since I was imprisoned, I have become more professional in criminal activities. I break the law in the prison in the heart of the law, so it is much easier for me to commit crimes outside. When I can transfer drugs from one section of the prison to another section fearlessly under the close control of guards from morning to evening with no chance of escape, transferring drugs outside is as simple as drinking water. (Male participant, ten years of incarceration)

After the few months I was in the prison, I got used to the circumstances and was not scared anymore. So, I started all the habits and behaviors I had before I was incarcerated. All criminal behaviors get repeated there. Everything formed again with the same quality but with the one exception that I was in prison and not in society anymore. We found drugs through any possible paths in the prison. (Male participant, eight years of incarceration)

Criminals with short-term sentences, such as petty drug offences, are not welcome to socialize with long-term inmates or to participate in prison activities (e.g., religion classes, sewing classes, etc.); however, they will grow familiar with the criminal lifestyle in cases of reoffence.

> For someone who spends a lot of time constantly in prison, prisons' rules become more stable in his mind. Even those who were incarcerated 10 times in their life and were incarcerated for a short period each time become gradually the same as us who were murderers, drug traffickers, or burglars. I mean, finally at the eleventh time, they were incarcerated because of murder, and they were sentenced to death. Then, such men found a status in the prison. (Male participant, seven years of incarceration)

Those petty drug offenders who have no intention of engaging in the prison criminal culture are not even considered human; they serve as the pariahs of the social hierarchy. This lack of a defined identity and sense of belonging to a specific group make short-term inmates the most vulnerable group to be exposed to the persistently unstable dynamics of the prison environment.

> I did not learn anything in the prison, neither criminal activities nor carpet weaving. There was not any spot for me. There were prisoners who were there for 10 or even 20 years who always participated in these types of classes with their fellows. They not only never asked me to come, but also if I wanted to, they would not let me in. Nobody counted on us. I did not talk to anybody because they did not even see me. We did not learn anything about the criminal activities because those groups and gangs did not talk to us. In return, when the boss changed, we were the first group who had to obey her new rules. (Female participant, one year of incarceration)

Regardless of whether it is desired, low level drug offenders are exposed to the toxic atmosphere in the prison (recriminalization) and various drugs (re-drugization). If a prisoner's drug of choice is unavailable (some drugs are rare and under direct control of the leaders, meaning buyers require strong connections and networks to access them) or unaffordable, they would switch to another drug or multiple substances. As such, these prisoners can become polydrug users depending on the accessibility and availability of drugs.

> I used opium and heroin, but I became familiar with methamphetamine in the prison. (Female participant, one year of incarceration)

> I was addicted to crack, but once I got released, I started injecting heroin. (Female participant, three years of incarceration)

Although Moradi et al. (2015) have highlighted the encouraging effects of prison-based methadone maintenance treatment to abate drug use and shared injections, the prevalence of various drugs beyond methadone was consistently noted and relayed by the participants. Even drug-free or recovering inmates also registered to receive methadone to combat anxiety and stress.

> I tried methadone in prison for the first time, because methamphetamine was 10 times more expensive than outside. Once I was released, I started to use methadone and methamphetamine simultaneously. (Female participant, three years of incarceration)

Although in-prison rehabilitation and treatment programs have never been emphasized or enhanced, a small number of prisoners have responded to the limited rehabilitation programs that specifically target addiction which seldom act as turning points. For instance, NA plays a significant role in the spiritual transformation of some prisoners, while the coexistence of the criminal subculture and NA subculture in the penal world exposed people in recovery to multiple identities. NA delivers a weekly program in the prison which is contiguous to their exterior rehabilitation centers. Usually, NA members in recovery with incarceration histories serve as the volunteers who present the program in prison. Neither correctional officers nor prisoners believed that NA principles were practiced by or inspired prisoners. Some violent criminals, however, changed their lives forever by participating in NA sessions.

The Dehumanization Ceremony   67

Guards did not believe in the function of NA in prison. They told us that prisoners do not understand the NA principles. (Male participant, nine years of incarceration)

In our section, there were 400 prisoners, and fewer than 10 prisoners attended the program. In fact, from those 10 prisoners, just three of them came to the program every week, and the rest of them came rarely. Prisoners are not well-informed about the principles of the program unless they attend the class. In fact, making different rumors and jokes around NA holds some prisoners back from attending this program. We made a joke about the NA meetings and the members in the prison. Instead of Narcotics Anonymous, we called them Soldier Anonymous. I did not attend any NA meetings in the prison as I was afraid of being sent to the forced labor camp. Some prisoners heard of NA's influence in quitting drugs, and thus they decided to attend the sections. (Male participant, seven years of incarceration)

Inmates in recovery, practicing the subculture of NA, generate a contradictory climate; prisoners simultaneously practice NA principles and combat the criminal subculture which permeates through all aspects of prison life. In doing so, they constantly define and redefine new statements for their daily activities which were previously part of a prison subculture. This leads to the formulation of a brand-new life statement, which possesses curtailed interest and followers in the penal system.

It was a well-known idiom in the prison that "even the gazelle does not feed his child" (nobody cares about anybody) in the prison; however, we as NA members in the prison attempted to encourage prisoners not to return to the prison again. We actually tried to expand their horizons in the prison. I was a manager in one cell in the prison; I told all the prisoners in the cell that nobody has a right to smoke even one cigarette in this cell. I told them on any occasion that you are not allowed to fight, just have a dialogue. They were not allowed to sell drugs in the cell. All of them must respect other cellmates' rights. I practiced all NA principles in the prison. Also, the number of former drug users who overcame

68   Life on Drugs in Iran

addiction in prison is no more than 1 or 2 out of 400 inmates. (Male participant, seven years of incarceration)

Although, as Crewe (2005) states, using substances can be considered "a largely individualistic response" to alleviate the pain of prison life, it is a point of departure to enhance social capital. More specifically, as Mjåland (2016, 159) states, using substances has "inclusionary and exclusionary functions." The essence of a considerable percentage of social interactions in the penal world is based on drugs. Consequently, drug withdrawal inspired by NA programs within prisons is not easily accepted, and the quality and quantity of social relationships can be entirely modified and replaced due to such a sudden departure from the norm. As Crewe (2005) postulates, inmates who quit drugs during their sentences have different social experiences of imprisonment.

> I became a part of an association in the prison where I could share my thoughts and feelings with them. It was called NA. I had several friends and cellmates in the prison, and we did not have any problems with each other after I participated in NA meetings. I was sick of my friends, and I could not stand them anymore. Once I quit drugs, I remember, I did not know what I was supposed to do with my friends. Every time I came back from the NA sessions, they surrounded me and offered me drugs. They told me to come to use drugs. Fortunately, I was trained by NA to say NO simply and immediately refusing this request. All the prisoners are sick of using drugs, and they have lost everything already in their life, but they could not quit that. My friends did not fight with me during the rehabilitation process in the prison, because I know that they wanted to stop using drugs, but they could not. (Male participant, nine years of incarceration)

According to interlocutors, NA members in prison restore relationships with family members who had excluded them due to their addiction. In fact, some family members, after resuming relationships with their loved ones, begin to support them financially to affirm and respect their decision to recover. Many of the lost connections and ties inside the prison community after withdrawal can be substituted by repairing relationships

The Dehumanization Ceremony   69

with family and friends outside the prison. According to Wacquant (2002, 388), prison is often viewed as a "distortive and wholly negative" force, while one can also consider it "as a stabilizing and restorative force for relations already deeply frayed by the pressures of life and labor at the bottom of the social edifice."

In addition to the NA program, inmates serving long-term sentences are often provided with life skills programs designed to educate them on emerging social and cultural changes in society. Although this education and preparation prior to release assists prisoners to readapt to the norms of society, many inmates still experience a culture shock after their release.

> When I got incarcerated, I was just 20 years old. The society was not the same, and also I was so young to be incarcerated and locked in a closed building for 10 years. I did not know anything about relationships between men and women, and once I wanted to figure it out, I murdered someone when I was high, and I got imprisoned. The society got turned upside down for 10 years. The only thing that kept me updated somehow, especially regarding boy/girl relationships, was the life skills class that was held in the prison. Prisoners such as I who were incarcerated at such sensitive ages who did not get a chance to figure out and practice social skills were trained in those educational classes in the prison. They constantly repeated the fact that opposite sex relationships have changed dramatically, and if you see unmarried boys and girls in the street who are hanging out freely, do not lose your control, and do not overreact, because this phenomenon is getting more normal than in the past, I mean 13 years ago . . . once I arrived at my parent's place and realized they have a satellite dish to watch western movies and listen to the music, I throw the satellite dish out of the window. Still I don't let them to fix it [sic]. Despite all training in the social classes in the prison, I was still shocked by all those differences. (Male participant, ten years of incarceration)

Two Sides of the Same Coin

High-status criminals are equivalent to correctional officers with regards to their authority to monitor and manage the prison system. Correctional officers voluntarily deliver the responsibilities of the prison management to high-status inmates who have gained enough legitimacy to mitigate violence, which otherwise portends chaos. Although trust is a tenuous concept in the prison community, guards do trust prisoners to be managed by their peers who exert influence and power throughout the prison. Given the prevalence of drug dependency in prison, drug traffickers have considerable influence through their charisma, which is directly rooted in their trade. They are an invaluable asset, allowing correctional officers to maintain correctional facilities without constant intervention.

> I did not see guards in the prison [because] the prisoners manage the prison themselves. (Male participant, ten years of incarceration)

> I saw guards just once a week, and the inmates with longer sentences managed the prison. I did not see any managers of the prison. Even in a case of fighting, correctional officers do not tend to interfere. (Male participant, three years of incarceration)

The reciprocal relationships between drug traffickers and correctional officers facilitate the flow of drugs into the prison. The absolute cooperation between prisoners and guards creates a mutually lucrative scenario that yields profit for both parties. Virtually all guards who illicitly cooperate in the drug business do so for financial purposes to afford their desired lifestyle.

> Even the employees and guards delivered drugs into the prison to earn money. They earned a lot of money by transferring drugs. The money they earned was much more than their salaries. It is one source of money. Guards deliver drugs to prison and make huge amounts of money. By delivering 50 grams of heroin, which cost $35 USD outside [the prison], they earn $350 USD inside [the prison]. (Male participant, eight years of incarceration)

Although financial intentions are a crucial component of drug compromises with prisoners, inmates skillfully deceive and manipulate guards periodically to gain sympathy or evoke compassion to their own ends.

The Dehumanization Ceremony   71

We forced guards to deliver to the prison whatever we wanted [sic]. We told them that we were here for years, and you must understand us. In the end, we made them emotional. We found a way to deliver drugs to the prison; for example, we would drop something in the bathrooms to cause clogs and then when the plumber came to the prison, we made friends with him. That was one way to persuade someone from the outside to bring drugs for us because they did not usually physically inspect them. I remember we persuaded a guard to bring vodka for us in the prison, because again they were not physically searched. (Male participant, seven years of incarceration)

Since wealthy prisoners who are high-status criminals (e.g., drug traffickers) are considered a financial pillar of the prison by providing essential accommodations (e.g., TV, carpet, radio, blanket, mattress, etc.) for the prisoners, they are treated respectfully and considered trustworthy negotiation partners by correctional officers.

You received respect from judges and guards if you were incarcerated for fraud of one hundred million toman. (Male participant, eight years of incarceration)

The reciprocal relationships between inmates and guards are not limited to financial interests or deception, as prisoners in exceptional situations received sincere sympathy and assistance from the wardens and correctional officers. In general, prisoners on death row are treated affectionately by guards. On the day of execution, correctional officers often attempt to abrogate the prisoner's sentence of capital punishment by asking the plaintiff for forgiveness. Whenever possible, they even provide opportunities for prisoners to leave the constraints of the prison to convince the plaintiff to forego the death penalty sentence.[5]

5. A similar theme is shown in the film "Beautiful City," directed by multi-award-winning filmmaker Asghar Farhadi in 2004. Akbar is the main character of this film. He committed murder at the age of sixteen and was sentenced to the death penalty. When he

72 Life on Drugs in Iran

The prosecutor released me based on his own promise to give me the opportunity to ask for the forgiveness of the plaintiff. (Male participant, nine years of incarceration)

One of the rituals which is popular among guards before execution is searching to find the family of the victim and begging them not to allow the prisoner to be executed. (Male participant, nine years of incarceration)

Some guards cry with all their hearts when innocent prisoners are executed, and sometimes guards devote a lot of time to delaying the execution of one prisoner with the hopes of getting the satisfaction of the plaintiff. (Male participant, seven years of incarceration)

On the one hand, correctional officers cooperate with prisoners in a mutually beneficial manner and facilitate their release, even if they are on death row; on the other, informants are recruited to disrupt prisoners' solidarity and intentionally jeopardize their social bonding. Through these informants, the culture of distrust intensifies and subsequently dissolves the sense of solidarity. Any potential solidarity or camaraderie between prisoners is stifled once it has been acknowledged. The informants are additionally recruited to deliver confidential information. A panopticon (Foucault 1977) makes the inmates feel constantly monitored, even in their own beds. Prison is organized through invisible agents of correctional officers (i.e., high-status criminals and informants) who trade information for the sake of their essential needs. They function as surveillance of all social activities, sowing instability, distrust, and uncertainty among inmates.

Snitches were set up by guards to decrease the solidarity between prisoners. If a prisoner gets powerful day by day in the prison, snitches

---

reaches age eighteen, the sentence legally can be carried out; thus he is transferred to the prison and awaits his execution. Meanwhile, a correctional officer in the rehabilitation center, along with Akbar's friend, try to gain the consent of Akbar's plaintiff to stop the execution, providing an opportunity for Akbar to pay *qisas* instead of being executed; https://www.imdb.com/title/tt0424434/.

received commands from wardens to spread rumors to ruin his reputation to decrease his power. (Male participant, ten years of incarceration)

Another defined duty of the recruited informants is to prevent kings from achieving excessive authority in prison, as this can lead to solidarity among inmates and promote collective actions. Following this strategy, the informants initiate the spread of rumors against the king to undermine their status or arrange a scheme to incriminate them. In such cases, informants and guards collaborate to trap the most influential prisoner by challenging his competency and legitimacy through subversive tactics. Informants are assigned to disrupt the growing trust and solidarity among prisoners, either by disclosing information to guards or by flailing false accusations designed to attack a target's reputation.

In the prison, there were some prisoners who became powerful during the time of incarceration. They committed violent crimes outside in the society and inside of the prison. Also, they transferred drugs from the prison to the outside and from the outside to the prison with assistance of guards and managers of the prison. There were so powerful that they had personal and family information on all involved managers and guards in case of disobedience. They were like a mafia; they managed drug trafficking from Shiraz to Zahedan. The warden of the prison realized that most of the guards and managers were involved in this situation, so they decided to spread the rumor that guns were being delivered into the prison. The rumors were spread by snitches, and then police enforcement came to search for the guns. First, they started searching their rooms, and the enforcement guards offended them greatly by searching every spot and separating prisoners into different cells. That was like a spark, as big fighting happened between the police and those prisoners. Police enforcement shot all six prisoners right in their own cell. Since then, managers have been cautious regarding prisoners who have the potential to become powerful in the prison. They started to recruit snitches to prevent the same situation from happening. (Male participant, ten years of incarceration)

4

NA

Stretching Normality

Narcotics Anonymous originated from the US Alcoholics Anonymous program of the late 1940s, with the first NA meeting held in Los Angeles in 1950. In 2021, there were 76,075 NA weekly meetings worldwide (NAWS 2021, 4). NA is one of the most effective voluntary recovery programs (Kaskutas 2009; Kelly et al. 2008; Robinson et al. 2009; White 2010).

The first Iranian NA group was established by Foruhar Tashvighi in 1994. Foruhar used substances for twenty years and recovered through the NA program while in the United States. Upon his return to Iran, he organized an NA group named *Anjoman-e Motadan-e Gomnam* (the society of anonymous addicts). Today, NA delivers a twelve-step program[1] and members are assigned a sponsor who is in recovery. Although NA is

---

1. (1) We admitted that we were powerless over our addiction, that our lives had become unmanageable. (2) We came to believe that a power greater than ourselves could restore us to sanity. (3) We made a decision to turn our will and our lives over to the care of God as we understood Him. (4) We made a searching and fearless moral inventory of ourselves. (5) We admitted to God, to ourselves, and to another human being the exact nature of our wrongs. (6) We were entirely ready to have God remove all these defects of character. (7) We humbly asked Him to remove our shortcomings. (8) We made a list of all persons we had harmed, and became willing to make amends to them all. (9) We made direct amends to such people wherever possible, except when to do so would injure them or others. (10) We continued to take personal inventory and when we were wrong promptly admitted it. (11) We sought through prayer and meditation to improve our conscious contact with God as we understood Him, praying only for knowledge of His will for us and the power to carry that out. (12) Having had a spiritual awakening as a result

Christian in origin, this did not impact participants' perspectives regarding NA in Iran in this present study. Many refused to identify their religious affiliation, believing instead in a "higher power."

Despite lacking proper treatment supervision, a growing number of drug treatment camps (illegal camps in particular) are absorbing an abundance of individuals who use substances in order to facilitate their recovery from drug addiction. However, the missions of drug treatment NGOs are not restricted to drug withdrawal. The respective NGOs indirectly break the cycle of humiliation and hatred of people who use substances by providing facilities and education and by humanizing people subject to substance use as dignified and capable of self-governance in society. Additionally, these institutions expand the definition of an ordinary citizen by treating those with histories of substance use humanely and by taking care of their essential needs (e.g., shelter, food, condoms, needles, etc.). Therefore, they try to progressively eliminate the concept of addiction use as taboo, though it is still manipulated by the security-oriented approach of the state.

Despite challenges related to registering NA as an NGO (i.e., according to one NA member, "since all people who use substances are welcomed to attend NA meetings regardless of their religion and ethnicity, it causes problems to officially register NA as an NGO because of its openness to everyone"), NA is not heavily inspected or monitored by any governmental bodies since it "uses abstinence-based methods" and "emphasizes readily endorsed cultural values" (Christensen 2011, 189). NA members are being equipped with the skills to restore their status in society and among their family members. The societal perception of those who use or have used substances is ameliorated through organizing open meetings that allow drug-free citizens, especially family and friends of those in recovery, to get involved in their beloved's recovery path while getting familiar with the treatment process, rather than marginalizing the issue of addiction. Thus, expanding the activities of NA and other treatment-oriented NGOs blurs

---

of these steps, we tried to carry this message to addicts, and to practice these principles in all our affairs.

76   Life on Drugs in Iran

the boundaries between the normal and perilous, as well as normalcy and deviancy; however, the impact of the program cannot penetrate the dominant securitization approach underpinning society. In the present study, four categories were extracted from the data to explain the subculture of NA in Iran: (1) Horizontal Networks, (2) Restricted and Exclusive Trust, (3) Constructing and Reconstructing Identities, and (4) Gender-Based Reintegration.

Horizontal Networks

NA groups are commonly comprised of several hierarchies: the steering committee (including the treasury), the area service committee, the regional service committee, and the world service office. However, NA is considered a fellowship by its members, with a bottom-up authority structure. Those serving on each committee are considered trusted servants who are neither dictatorial nor delegators; rather, they listen to others and are available to help, direct, and advise. These representatives occupy a crucial role in problem sharing and solving but are not involved in policymaking or enforcing decisions (Peyrot 1985). Despite the various levels within the hierarchy, all NA members have the prerogative to serve on each committee and be a leader. One of the most important criteria for selecting representatives is humility in terms of one's own strengths and limitations. Newcomers to NA are imbued with a special status in meetings; they are considered the heart of NA.

> NA survives through newcomers. If they do not come, NA meetings will die. (Male participant, eighteen years in NA)

The crucial role of newcomers in the survival of NA meetings penetrates all aspects of the program. When newcomers arrive, they are embraced with affection. People who use substances are excluded from society before joining NA. Thus, the emotional expression and moral support of NA, especially from long-term members, is highly appreciated. Despite being rejected and isolated by society and loved ones, they are humanized and accepted in NA. Living and struggling with the constant fear of arrest and exclusion forces them to avoid having a social life. However, NA is the first social community for virtually all members in which they are respected, valued, loved, and trusted.

> I told everyone that I'm an addict in the first session while I was in physical pain due to drug withdrawal. In response, everyone clapped for me for five minutes. As they were clapping, it was like injecting a painkiller inside me. I could not believe that I was being loved by those people. (Male participant, ten years in NA)

> Feeling discriminated against by our family members pushed us to take drugs. In this atmosphere, all of us are equal. We are all respected here. Long-term recovering addicts understand other members even more; besides, they are all equal to us, and there is no best and worst among us. We all have the same problem, and we are here for the same reasons. (Male participant, ten years in NA)

> Nobody cared about me in my time of addiction. That was the first time that people were interested in my existence. Before, I thought I was not alive, I was dead. But the first time I was at an NA meeting, I realized that I'm alive. (Female participant, twelve years in NA)

There is a reciprocal, respectful relationship among NA members from the newcomers to the long-term members. Everyone in NA occupies a unique and respectful status, which requires detailed responsibilities and commitments with no hierarchical superiority.

> There is no hierarchy in NA. The oldest members of NA receive respect, and in return, they respect new members most. (Female participant, five years in NA)

> Although now I am a ten-year member of NA, there is no room for being superior. We all are the same in NA. (Male participant, ten years in NA)

Physical, behavioral, and psychological symptoms of addiction increase the level of mental distress and fear of being arrested or stigmatized

78   Life on Drugs in Iran

in society. Most avoid communicating with others or attending social gatherings, and often choose to appear in public at night to be less distinguishable. The fear of being labeled as an addict (*motad*) and the inherent shame stemming from their physical deterioration follow them like a shadow—even as they attend an NA meeting for the very first time.

> I did not go to the street during day. I always went out at night. I did not want to be seen by others. People realized that I'm an addict, and it changed their perception and the way of speaking to me. The first time I went to the NA meeting, my physical appearance was awful. I did not even have clean clothes to wear. I remember a time when one of the NA members saw me at the entrance door. She loudly said, "Welcome, welcome my dear." She recognized me, and she realized that I'm an addict. I was scared and full of shame. I did not wear appropriate clothes, but that did not matter for them. They all hugged me and kissed me. They told me "Do not worry, everything is going to be fine." It was the first time that people hugged me and kissed me and accepted me as I was. (Female participant, twelve years in NA)

An important, unwritten rule requires NA members to wear casual outfits at NA meetings to avoid making anyone uncomfortable, especially newcomers. According to the interlocutors, NA is a space of equality and mutual respect based on shared experiences of addiction as a disease despite its diversity.

> We are not talking about how wealthy you are, and we are not wearing ties or any special clothes. We are wearing the most casual clothes in the meeting, even if we are a professor or businessman in society. The most important thing is to respect the feelings of the newcomers. If our appearance is different from the newcomers, they might feel uncomfortable or isolated here. Our physical appearance must convey the message to them that we are the same. We are all addicts. (Male participant, eight years in NA)

Principles such as "we don't care who you are; we care about the therapeutic value of one addict helping another" and "we are all equal when we sit together in NA meetings" are practiced every day among NA members to enhance the equality culture in the organization (Public Relation Handbook 2006, 6–7). However, the fact that this was not explicitly negotiated indicates a strong tendency toward being distinguishable through sponsorship and overseeing various NA activities. One of the NA members, in recovery for almost fourteen years, disclosed a pervasive tendency for popularity among long-term members.

> Yes, of course, [we are all equal] in the program. We all have the same objective. Nobody is higher or above anyone else. But . . . I had 150 [sponsees]. After accepting more and more [sponsees] I started to enjoy being seen and [recognized] in the meetings and among NA members. Lots of people nationwide started to hear about me and request [to be my sponsees]. Being cherished with different people made me powerful. It is not just me; I can name lots of people in the program who are power-hungry. They want to be recognized by others in the NA meetings. They want to be known by all women and men in NA. (Male participant, fourteen years in NA)

An eagerness to be recognizable and distinguished among NA members and in the society as a whole was noted to have trapped many long-term members while, in contrast, anonymity remains as one of the fundamental principles of NA.[2] One long-term NA member who agreed to participate in the study wrote back to me a very impressive letter: "Please accept my invitation and come to my place. I want to show you my life." For more than six months, he had stopped sponsoring new members since his wife had abandoned him. There was an empty home with books everywhere. He had been in recovery for nearly nine years and was a sponsor[3] (*rahnama*) for 250 NA members nationwide.

2. "[We] place the principle of anonymous, selfless giving before whatever personal desires we may have for recognition or reward" (NAWS 1993, 212).

3. An "NA sponsor is a member of Narcotics Anonymous, living our program of recovery, who is willing to build a special, supportive, one-on-one relationship with us. Most members think of a sponsor, first and foremost, as someone who can help us work the Twelve Steps of NA, and sometimes the Twelve Traditions and Twelve Concepts. Sponsors

I had a very happy life with my wife and child, but my wife left me because I had several young girl sponsees. First, NA returned my life to me, and then it took it back. I ignored the principles of NA by taking on that many sponsees. However, NA members intend to keep their anonymity, but it is bullshit. I was one of those who cannot stop getting more and more sponsees and becoming more popular and well known in NA. I thought because I read some books, have a sponsor who lives in a foreign country and have 9 years of experience in NA that I have the right to advise and make decisions for others. I saw a difference between myself and even you, who are a PhD student in a foreign country. You know why? The NA principles give this power, or it is better to say, this illusion, to me. Most NA members with long experience lose their anonymity and misuse this status by considering themselves beyond other people in the society. They do not accept anyone in the society. They tell themselves, "I was an addict, and then I got clean and started a spiritual transformation, so there is nothing that I have not experienced. I have experienced the worst things and then was rescued. Thus, I have a power over others." This is our justification. Even if nobody tells you this, it becomes your reality. Thus, I must stop accepting any new sponsees, so I can find myself to find out who I am. My wife was a nonaddict. She always told me that you are going to lose this game (my life) because of NA. She was right. I lost myself and my wife simultaneously.

A desire for social superiority extends beyond the scope of NA, and some long-term members consider themselves equivalent to psychologists and psychotherapists who consult on a broad range of issues and

---

share their experience, strength, and hope with their sponsees. Some describe their sponsor as loving and compassionate, someone they can count on to listen and support them no matter what. Others value the objectivity and detachment a sponsor can offer, relying on their direct and honest input even when it may be difficult to accept. Still others turn to a sponsor mainly for guidance through the Twelve Steps. A sponsor's role is not that of a legal advisor, a banker, a parent, a marriage counselor, or a social worker. Nor is a sponsor a therapist offering some sort of professional advice. A sponsor is simply another addict in recovery who is willing to share his or her journey through the Twelve Steps" (Narcotics Anonymous World Services).

recommend appropriate solutions. NA principles are considered an exclusive knowledge accessible to the NA members that is kept in strict secrecy from drug-free citizens. Being a member of the NA community is considered such a coveted privilege that perceived superiority over non-NA members becomes a faith.

> No, you got me wrong. I know how to resolve my family issues, because I'm equipped with NA principles. NA gave me a perspective. I am practicing principles that ordinary people are deprived of. My relatives and family ask for me when they have any problems and issues, and I resolve their challenges. (Female participant, ten years in NA)

NA members view themselves as a tight-knit group ("us") and drug-free citizens as "others." During interviews, they referred to me as an *adam-e adi* (ordinary). Most considered it a problem that I had not experienced addiction and was unfamiliar with the process of spiritual transformation through NA principles. During the interviews, some sarcastically reminded me that I do not understand their life and even questioned my research due to lack of addiction experiences.

> How can you understand NA's missions and principles when you have never touched heroin in your life? How can you understand how difficult it is to quit heroin and how NA fellows help each other on this road? You are not in the right place, Nahid. Change your route and go back. You have to be a member of NA to understand NA principles. (Male participant, nine years in NA)

Some prominent sponsors with long-term experience believed they possessed spiritual power over their family members, relatives, and friends to the extent that no one in their family can make any critical decision without their consultation. Members also believed that NA principles drive members toward the illusionary perception of superiority against society. One well-known NA fellow quoted his wife's trepidation about NA:

> She says to me every single day that the worst part of being an NA member is that you think you are God and you know everything, and you act

as God. She told me that "you think you are superior because you are an NA member, but in reality, you do not know anything, and you are like *tabl-e to khali* (empty vessels make the most sound)."

Restricted and Exclusive Trust

Shakable Trust

The prevalence of mistrust is a common feature of the organizations covered in this study (governmental bodies and NGOs alike). In fact, the crisis of trust in Iran was confirmed even by the results on nationwide representative surveys. According to a World Values Survey conducted in 2005, 88.7 percent of Iranians declared they must be careful in dealing with others. The level of trust in the country, 10.5 percent, is two and a half times less than the average for the World Values Survey general sample (25.4 percent). The atmosphere in which people who use substances struggle before joining NA combines stigma, shame, exclusion, and isolation; after joining NA meetings, members' egregious treatment in society at large is made apparent to them.[4] Most participants enter NA meetings with uncertainty and hesitation. They cannot believe that the twelve-step program leads to moral, emotional, and physical transformations. The very first pervasive assumption among all newcomers was that attendees of the NA meetings are engaged in a deceitful facade to elicit a confession for their committed crimes and subsequently, get arrested by law enforcement. Despite pervasive medical interventions targeting addiction in Iran, for those who use substances, the discourse on criminalization dominates their lives even in NA meetings. During their first few months, almost all NA newcomers are subject to anxiety and stress; however, the internalized fears and precarious essence of trust are partially replaced by the confidence of living freely with no fear of being arrested.

---

4. According to Behrouzan's (2010, 325) study about HIV and AIDs in prisons, "stigma was the first obstacle to providing medical support; the majority of these patients had been disowned by their families and communities."

In the society, we always struggle with the fear of being monitored or arrested. But in NA, there is no monitoring. We are afraid of being judged or being arrested in the society, but in NA you're outside this situation. It's exactly the boundaries between NA and the society, and it's very specific. Thus, people are forced to play a dual character. NA is a circle, and you should not expect nonjudgmental behaviors in society outside the NA community. (Male participant, eighteen years in NA)

It was unbelievable that all those happy and beautiful women were addicted or even committed slight crimes before. I thought that all of them were social workers and wanted to arrest me. But even though I thought this way, I could not stop seeing them every day. I hated drugs, and I told myself that it does not matter, and I do not care. It is enough for me to get clean no matter what. The worst-case scenario is that I will be arrested, but at least I got clean. (Female participant, eight years in NA)

Full disclosure in NA meetings was hindered by painful memories of being stigmatized and isolated and of experiences encompassing forced hospitalizations by the member's family in the name of treatment.

Fear of disclosing in front of others always followed me. The first three years, I did not tell the whole story about my life, as I could not trust anyone. How could you possibly trust anyone in that circumstance? While every member of the society was ready to punish you in their own way, one with prison, one with a compulsory treatment, one with exclusion. (Female participant, twelve years in NA)

Disclosure is more complicated for female members. Although addiction is stigmatized despite gender, women in a patriarchal society such as Iran are subject to double standards—particularly that addiction acutely jeopardizes their principal role as a wife and mother. Thus, the fear and shame of multiple forms of stigmatization deter women from seeking treatment. For those who overcome the fear of stigmatization and engage with NA, they continually struggle with the disclosure process in the meetings. Violating society's definition of what constitutes an honorable and decent woman drives them to internalize their shame and fear.

84   Life on Drugs in Iran

> It was embarrassing for me to talk about my desire to have sexual rela-
> tionships. I could not talk about these desires loudly. I did not feel safe
> to discuss them. What would other members think of me if I told them
> that I had several sexual relationships with different men. I could not tell
> them that I lost my children. (Female participant, twelve years in NA)

However, people in recovery consider NA meetings as their sanctuary; a haven where they are provided with a serene, tranquil, and safe atmosphere in stark contrast to their familial atmosphere where there is a tendency for them, especially women, to be treated as social pariahs. NA is a safe shelter in which the sense of belonging to the community, regardless of background, is offered warmly. Women often consider themselves asylum seekers at NA recovery meetings.

> For me, NA is literally a second home. I have the same calmness that I
> have in my own house. Sometimes I feel bad at my house, for example, if
> my husband is saying something bad to me and I get upset or my daugh-
> ter says something that deeply worries me, then I go to my second home,
> where I have peace and safety. I have a place that belongs to me. My
> name is not carved there, but my friends there are waiting for me there.
> It is a comfortable and safe place to talk, and other members listen very
> well and carefully. I often say that if I explain my feelings to my mom,
> maybe she will bite me and say you are a crazy girl. But I know there's a
> place where they listen to me and do not laugh at me. They understand
> and accept me with all my thoughts. I'm sick, and my illness is over-
> abundant. NA is the only place that helped me and where I could find
> my true self and my true personality. NA made me be another person.
> (Female participant, five years in NA)

Most participants assumed they could find safety and security while choosing to forego authenticity and transparency. However, non-judgmental support for treatment in NA meetings provides the opportunity for members to share their life story despite reluctance and suspicion. Nevertheless, women in recovery are constantly subject to the criminalization discourse by NA recovering males. Although female members

Stretching Normality 85

occasionally have a brief introduction in the open NA meetings, being stigmatized and judged by their male counterparts keep them cautious and silent.

> Men in NA think of us as untrustworthy [humans] who can sexually seduce men. As someone who has poly-sexual relationships and left kids and husband behind . . . they prefer to not [be in contact with women members] as it might jeopardize their sobriety. Most [women] prefer to hide or be silent in front of men to not [be] judged. Addiction seems to have a different meaning for them [depending] on gender. (Female participant, nine years in NA)

It is worth noting that long-term members are supposed to be sponsors of those in recovery, regardless of gender. However, they rarely accept women as sponsees (*rahjo*) due to the prevalence of misjudgments and stigma regarding intergender relationships in NA. Prejudice is not the sole reason that deters recovering men from sponsoring recovering women; avoidance of issues (e.g., emotional relationships) that may jeopardize NA principles and delay the recovery process is also a factor.

> I have had three sponsors since I entered NA, and the last one was a man. He is one of the most experienced NA members, and I tried hard to convince him to be my sponsor. He was in NA for about 20 years, and I need someone with that much experience. I did not find a woman in recovery with that much experience in NA. Thus, I decided to talk with and convince him. I told him how much I needed his help and recovery experience. After several months, he accepted my request under several conditions. (Female participant, nine years in NA)

> I had a really handsome sponsor for more than 4 years, and our relationship left the main road, I mean working on the twelve steps. I said goodbye to him after 4 years, but the point is that it delayed my recovery process. It is important to be cautious about choosing the sponsor, and you must be careful if you choose a man as a sponsor. (Female participant, twelve years in NA)

86   Life on Drugs in Iran

Restricted Trust

While the radius of trust does not encompass the entire sphere of NA members' lives, it does cover several common and shared goals (e.g., sobriety). Trusting relationships toward restoring and recovery are exercised by NA members to overcome the distrust from society at large. However, members' limited trust typically revolves around recovery goals, having been advised by long-term members not to trust matters beyond shared goals. Even trust between sponsors and their sponsored NA members is defined and restricted to NA principles.

> The relationship between the sponsor and sponsee is restricted to the NA principles. Their relationship must circulate around their common target, no more. If it goes beyond this, they face several problems. (Male participant, eighteen years in NA)

I was invited to a private social gathering of NA members. The sponsor of the group was a well-known NA member with nearly twenty years of sobriety. While other members were barbequing and preparing a dinner table, we found a quiet spot to converse. In the first few minutes of discussion, he brought up the fragile and restricted nature of trust in the NA community. He described trust among NA members as a bridge, which ends in a long valley with abundant warning signs. One of the most important injunctions for him pertained to socializing with NA members' families. He believes that recovering NA members are still dependent on substances and criminals who have not given up their previous habits, and these dormant habits undermined his trust.

> If I lend money to an NA member, and he did not return his debt, it is not his fault. In fact, his act is not unpredictable. It is my fault for trusting him beyond our common goals. We join NA to be clean and stay clean, and for this reason, we have trusted each other, shared our experiences, and been transparent about our history. For this specific reason, we must trust; otherwise, nothing will happen regarding the addiction issue in our lives. We do not get hurt by trusting each other regarding

addiction issues, but we had a case of a person who started to have family relationships with other NA members, which caused several dilemmas and challenges in the family. In fact, the meaning that NA members get from trust is completely incorrect. Trust is based on principles and is within the framework of the NA system. We are two people, and we have the same disease. We have a target, addiction, and we want to get rid of it, thus we can build trust around the common points. My best friends are all NA members, but we do not have family and financial relationships, because if we have these kinds of relationships we will be hurt. The experiences of other members reveal the fact that all NA members get hurt by starting relationships beyond NA goals, because these are the boundaries between society and NA. Relationships in society are based on mistrust, so expanding our relationships to society will be a big mistake. I have several friends in NA whom I trust 100 percent, but I will never ask them for anything beyond NA, because for sure that would be a mistake. I see that all my friendships in NA are as strong as before because I did not step beyond the NA territory with them. I trust all NA members around the NA programs (e.g., rehabilitation process) but not more. I even mentioned in public meetings with NA members that I would never let my daughter marry an NA member. My point is that I do not believe in NA members to that extent for one to be my daughter's husband. So many people consult with me about marrying NA members, and I changed their mind and told them that if you want to give up your daughter's life, let her marry an NA member. But, on the other hand, I trust them in the rehabilitation process and believe that nobody can help us in this matter but other NA members. The point is that they are all addicts, murderers, thieves, drug dealers, or traffickers, and irresponsible people in society. They are so unstable; you cannot count on them. The possibility that they will engage in antisocial behaviors or crimes is really high. We have unstable personalities. We sound like good people, but the reality of our life shows something else. We have enormous challenges, and we struggle with our instabilities constantly. If you talk with some members of NA, you may think he is a prophet; he acts and talks in a way that cannot be found in any book. He learned all those principles and spiritualty from NA, but he sneakily uses drugs. How can anyone trust us? You cannot trust any NA member, let alone members in treatment camps or prisons. There is no trust beyond the NA principles and goals. We dedicate our time and energy to NA members only for our common goals. I trust them in the framework of NA, but if he asks me to be my guarantor in court, I would definitely reject him.

Exclusive Trust

Securitization and crime-oriented policies and programs toward addiction have marginalized people who use substances to the extent that even those interacting with them in society, including family members, are considered unprincipled expatriates. The distrustful culture makes the process of reintegration extremely challenging; socializing and communicating with drug-free citizens, including family, friends, and relatives, accelerates the process of returning to a life of normalcy; however, the majority of NA members, especially women, do not have this advantage.

> All people in the society, in your family talk to you, and it seems that you are their best friend, but once you go away, they start to go back to biting and assaulting you. This is my view about our society and our people. I do not trust them. They are not honest for even one second. They are just lying and bluffing. But in NA, we call each other during depressing moments, and we just listen with no judging and no monitoring and no threatening. We are working and supporting each other like a team. Trust means you feel safe to talk to me about whatever you are concerned about without even a slight sign of danger. I talk with my sponsor about anything, and he never judges me. I am talking to you now because my sponsor guaranteed you. You know what I mean. When I was addicted, either I trusted as much as I got hurt, or I could not make any friends. I thought that all people in society are liars, from employees of all governmental organizations to my children's teachers at school. The NA principles taught me how to trust people. I learned how to trust in NA. There is no reason to talk to anybody about my past and backgrounds, and I adjust my distance with people in society now. You cannot trust people in society. You can trust people in NA, as they are always there for me. (Female participant, four years in NA)

Preliminary attempts to build stable and trusting relationships between people in recovery and drug-free citizens are facilitated by two NA reintegration arrangements: open meetings and compensation. Through open meetings, drug-free citizens, including friends and family members of those in recovery, are invited to gather and celebrate their loved ones' "clean anniversary." Publicly sharing life experiences succors NA members to combat their fears and embarrassment, which permeated through their lives for years. It also provides drug-free citizens with the opportunity to witness a medical-oriented approach. Additionally, through the compensation process, most NA members rebuild their connections with relatives and friends, enhancing social bonds and social capital, which in turn helps drug-free citizens to become more comfortable in restoring relationships with their loved ones in recovery. This occurs by way of comprehending the treatment process and monitoring their behavioral and physical transformations. It is worth noting that although the scope of trust has its own limitations and restrictions among NA members and their communications with drug-free citizens, the process of building and developing trust occurs gradually. Progressive, mutual trust among those in recovery and drug-free citizens takes place steadily through the practice of NA principles in daily life.

However, I received numerous complaints from family members regarding the multiple identities of NA members. Most NA members practice the NA principles exclusively with NA fellows. They designed two life scenarios after attending NA meetings: one for communication with drug-free citizens (*mardom-e adi*), especially their families, and another pertaining to their NA fellows. This demarcation in behavior stems from the exclusive and restricted trust culture in the NA program which can be explained by the dominant criminalization approach in society toward addiction. A wife of one of the most popular NA members was frustrated by the multiple identities of her husband.

> You cannot believe how my husband treats the other members in NA, as his behavior is not comparable with the people he deals with every day. Sometimes, when he is talking with his NA friends, I think he has

90   Life on Drugs in Iran

turned into another person so much that I don't recognize him. He becomes a completely different person and advises them in a way that is the complete reverse of his own behavior with us and with other people in society. One day, I went out for a picnic with my husband and children. We started to talk about a topic which I do not remember now, but he shouted while talking and acted unfairly. Meanwhile, one of the NA members called and asked my husband a question because my husband was his sponsor. My husband advised him to be fair and kind toward others, solve problems in peace, etc. Actually, we as his family have witnessed this hypocritical behavior several times. Most of the time, the way he acts with people in society is 100 percent in conflict with his behaviors toward NA members. (Family member)

Despite perceived improvements in the lives of those in recovery, pivoting to other forms of addiction can become another barrier that undermines trustful relationships between family and NA members. In some cases, family of NA members believe that their loved one has substituted their substance use for other vices, such as sex, overeating, oversleeping, or smoking.

You see my wife; I cannot talk in front of her because she will start fighting with me. You know why? Because she believes that we are not recovering addicts in NA; we are just turning our addiction to other things such as sex, sleep, eating food, or smoking cigarettes. (Male participant, fifteen years in NA)

The dependency on reciprocated emotional and informational support to endure the healing process is a widely accepted phenomenon in NA. However, excessive dependency on companionship and the NA recovery support network complicates the personal lives of NA members. It is assumed that exclusive friendships with NA peers are the most suitable alternative to substance use; this practice of camaraderie is obstinately prioritized above all else.

He cannot leave without his NA fellows; he has to see them every day. How [can] you can say that they are not [addicts]. Of course, it is not addiction, it is not problematic for their health, but it put their family relations in jeopardy. We, families, thought we [were] set free from the drugs, now we [are] stuck in NA. No specific schedule, 24/7, are being in contact with NAs [sic]. It is another addiction. Nothing has been solved, Nothing. Just they have jumped from one step to another one. We are still suffering. NA is another type of drug. They have to be in constant contact with NA, all their friends are NA fellows. The bottom line is that they cannot live without NA. (Family member)

In the end, it is noteworthy to consider that NA members at least practice building trusting relationships, even if those relationships are restricted to the NA principles and drug-free citizens in society are excluded from taking part. Although establishing stable trustworthy relationships between NA members and drug-free families is an ongoing project, both parties are engaged and eager to resolve the issue, which is not the case for those who use substances and live on the street. They regularly came to the night drop-in center, a nongovernmental harm reduction center, and communicated with other clients. However, observation reflects that their relations were based on daily needs (e.g., food, clothes, a safe place to sleep). Although they were involved in several group activities such as cooking, drinking tea, and serving dinner, they preferred to remain reticent, and interactions were often wordless. The night drop-in center, surrounded with large brick walls, was an impervious shelter serving to protect homeless women who use substances from street violence at night. However, the constant and regular contact with other clients who struggled with the same challenges did not spark trusting relationships. The manager of the institution, who had used substances for seven years before her recovery, started working at the center while also being an active NA member. One night, the manager wanted to leave the center for thirty minutes. She told me:

Nahid, do not trust anyone. Just sit in my chair and do not listen to the bullshit they are going to tell you. Do not open the door and do not let anyone leave. If anyone goes out at this time of the night, you do not let them back. Be careful. Do not trust them at all.

However, those who participated in nongovernmental treatment and recovery camps were mostly involved in the NA twelve-step program and were practicing the principles in the camp. It was common that the managers of those camps were members of NA or at least had an NA representative in their camp to assist people in recovery. In contrast to the absence of trust in the night drop-in center, the treatment camps were almost entirely operated by people in recovery. I met the manager only once when collecting data at the center; the other times, those in recovery guided me to the interview room and encouraged the inhabitants to share their experiences, while managing and monitoring the whole procedure. As expressed by the camp manager:

> I leave the camp in the morning every day and come back at noon, and you would not believe that one of the recovering addicts who got clean here one year ago managed the camp during the time of my absence. I could trust those who are under the training of the NA program. They are practicing NA principles in the camp.

One of the illegal treatment camps applied NA principles despite using coercive methods, especially during the detoxification period. The camp was managed by an NA member who was a sponsor of fifteen other people in recovery at the camp. The trusting relationships between clients and the manager kept a wanted criminal clean, safe, and secure in the camp community, and facilitated having full support and attention regarding their legal conundrums. According to one of the participants in that camp:

> I trust the manager of the camp. He knows that I was under arrest, and he knows that I stole a lot of money, and the police were going to arrest me sooner or later. But he did not say one thing about my circumstances. He helped me to quit drugs and start the twelve-step program. He promised me that he would figure out and find a solution to help me with my criminal record but only on the condition that I stay clean. All my family members had left me, so he started to talk with them and convinced them to start communicating with me again. I trust him. He is like an angel for me.

Constructing and Reconstructing Identities

Interpreting the Identity

By attending twelve-step NA meetings, people in recovery experience a gradual transformation, a core change (Mahoney 1980), which is also referred to as a deep structural change (Arnkoff 1980). The participants affirmed that the temporal dimension of the transformation process does not occur instantaneously. The multiple identities of people in recovery reveal the fact that they are in interminable departure from appellations such as "diseased" to "criminal." By contributing to different services in the NA program, from chairing meetings to being a sponsor, and in fulfilling and practicing the tenets of NA, NA members distance themselves from their identity as a criminal and shift toward a self-perception of being afflicted or a patient. However, while members are continually engaged in the construction and reconstruction of their identity during the recovery phase, they do not meet the requirements of society's perception of a criminal, recovering addict, sick patient, or normal citizen. The identity of NA members is contested, dynamic and diverse, and the process of transformation involves NA members incorporating aspects of several novel identities into their own. The multiple identities, appearing to be fluid and often in conflict, are affected by gradual and endless phases of construction and reconstruction as members are influenced by the NA principles, NA fellows, and drug-free citizens (i.e., family members, spouses, friends, and colleagues). However, the first step toward the recovery pathway is a sense of acceptance of the addicted identity.

> By admitting that I am an addict, I have accepted reality for the first time in my life. I did not believe that I was an addict, as I always lived with this reality that I have control over my life and drugs. The first time I heard myself say it, something inside me was broken. That was the fake me that collapsed as soon as I called myself an addict. I cried so hard; I could not believe that I had finally called myself an addict. I accepted this reality. I accepted all the consequences of being an addict for the first time. I have always avoided this truth, but at that moment,

> I accepted myself. That was a relief. I finally accepted the reality. That was the first step that took 2 months for me to admit. During the very first meeting, I just cried and cried. The long-termers always advised me, "Please introduce yourself. Please talk to us." But I could not. The day that I was brave enough to say those words, all the fellows clapped their hands for me, and I cried. So, I am honest with myself and with others. Also, I accept reality now. (Female participant, twelve years in NA)

People who use substances, whether in a process of quitting or still suffering, are trapped in an endless struggle with society's predefined identities. The conflict does not disappear by merely joining NA; rather, the struggle becomes a triple contest between the addicted identity, the recovering identity, and the identity conceptualized by society. Even if people in addiction recovery internalize the addicted identity, the progressive contrast between the identity of the normal citizen and the NA recovering identity becomes an inseparable part of their lives. Although NA principles lead members to achieve a closer approximation of the normal citizen identity, the gap will remain. The full reintegration of the NA members to society is still questionable, especially among female NA members recovering from addiction. The contrast is an endless journey; people who use drugs have not totally lost their "normal" identity, yet are classified as criminals, addicts, or prostitutes (in the case of women). The NA twelve-step program helps participants shed these three identities, which otherwise paint them as social outcasts.

Females in recovery embark on a different journey than men. The constant struggle between the ex-convict identity, recovery identity, and in some cases prostitute identity, constrains them from achieving psychological equilibrium. Society has conjectured the notion that women who use substances violate social and cultural norms. It is apparent that the so-called war on drugs in Iran can be dubbed the "war against women." Despite extensive time spent in recovery programs, struggles between the different identities perpetually affect females in recovery. Even if they attempt to relieve their pain and alleviate their embarrassment and stigma, societal perceptions and stereotypes are quick to remind them of their arbitrary identities.

Testimony is the first stage of the twelve-step NA program that catalyzes the process of constructing a new self-perception to review, evaluate, and transpose undesirable identities and thereby plays a pivotal role in identity construction and reconstruction. By listening and sharing, the process of interpreting the former identity is facilitated. Additionally, finding common and similar experiences with peers assists them in constructing their new identity in connection with the NA community. In other words, the testimony bridges all three of the contested worlds: the former addicted self, the current in-recovery self, and the future drug-free self. The nonjudgmental, intrepid, and unmonitored testimony provides an opportunity for NA members to confidently interpret their former identities (i.e., criminal, addict, prostitute) and as time passes, gain control over them. The former socially undesirable and unacceptable identities which were previously a target for various stigmas and unsavory labels are gradually interchanged with the recovery identity, which is connected to the individual through a specific universal discourse. Although disclosure for the family members was impossible due to the constant process of exclusion and stigmatization, sharing similar stories of suffering through the testimonial process with the NA fellows creates a homogenized atmosphere where all members are equal.

> When I said in the meeting that I could not control my sexual tendencies toward the opposite sex, all of them understood me, but it was impossible to talk about my sexual desires among normal people, even my family members. They would kill me for sure. They do not understand me, because they do not know what an addiction is. Just us in NA, we know addiction best, and we know all the hidden parts of our disease. Each addict who enters NA reveals to us and reminds us of a part of our disease. (Female participant, one year in NA)

Interlocutors believe that since they occupy social statuses as pariahs in society, the only community willing to assist them is their peers. Promulgating this message to those who suffer using substances in all institutions, such as prisons and hospitals, is the most important commitment of each NA member.

> I send the NA message to drug addicts in the prison and in the hospital. They must know that they are not alone. They must know that we are all the same, and we are all equal. We all are not accepted in society and always feel that we are alone in the world. But we go to the institutions and let them know they can get clean, and they can have real and true friends. It is one of the biggest responsibilities I have committed to doing. (Male participant, five years in NA)

At NA meetings, there is a constant interplay between personal testimony, mutual understanding, and commitment. The all-inclusive NA recovery program emphasizes similarities rather than differences; repeating and listening to the same stories from almost all members reveal the commonalities in the addicted identity. Although most newcomers attempt to distinguish themselves from others during initial meetings, practicing and imitating the NA language creates harmony between all members regardless of distinctions in length of sobriety and gender. Long-term members and newcomers share their recovery stories constantly in joint meetings, which reminds them of the possibility of attaining recovery and of the downsides of addiction simultaneously. The homogeneity and harmony among NA members provide the opportunity for members to review their addict identity, and to create and practice their new identity.

The unmonitored and free inner group testimony creates the stage where people in recovery realize similarities and commonalities among the meticulously paved paths that the NA members have taken. This creates a sense of belonging to the community, as the isolated identity can be disclosed for the first time. The homogeneity and harmony between all in-recovery identities also increases the inner group's cohesion, solidarity, and mutual commitment. Through consistent participation and attendance of NA meetings, communication with NA fellows, involvement in NA events and activities, and practice of principles under guidance of sponsors, participants repeatedly recall their addicted identity. Although NA meetings are considered a home for members, constantly moving between multiple contexts and identities creates a nomadic obfuscated life where they have not settled into either identity.

Spiritual Transformation

Spiritual transformation has been studied in different forms and contexts, including addiction recovery (Blakeney et al. 2006; Dufault-Hunter 2012; McCoy et al. 2004, 2005; Neff and MacMaster 2005; Windsor and Shorkey 2010). A key component of the twelve-step recovery program is its spiritual dimension, regardless of the overarching religious context. Almost all members, from newcomers to long-term members, believe in the help of a "higher power" in the process of recovery. Most participants reported having experienced a gradual spiritual awakening in NA. Long-term members and sponsors emphasized the spiritual aspects of NA principles and encouraged the spiritual involvement of other members (especially, newcomers). According to Galanter et al. (2013, 1), "NA is self-designated as spiritual, rather than religious. It is not theistic as such, espousing God only as we understood him, thereby allowing for a flexible view of acceptance of a 'Higher Power,' with no rules as to how or who they believe their Higher Power is."

There is a strong connection between recovery and spiritual transformation in NA which is one of the integral components of constructing and reconstructing one's identity based on NA principles. The reference to a spiritual awakening and maturity is not based on religious practices but rather on the tendency to embrace acceptance and humility.

Admitting powerlessness over addiction and believing in a higher power are the triggers for the spiritual awakening of NA participants. The most important tool for spiritual growth or spiritual awakening is attending meetings and being constantly engaged in the discourse. The pivotal role of believing in a higher power (i.e., a connection with a power greater than oneself), interpreting the destructive identity through constant testimony (i.e., a connection with oneself), and caring for others (i.e., connections with others) in the path toward recovery is undeniable.

This spiritual awakening is a gradual process of loving, caring, accepting, trusting oneself and others, and revering a higher power as a replacement

98   Life on Drugs in Iran

for the lifestyle encumbered by addiction. Through their strong commitment toward the twelve-step program, those in recovery are no longer self-centered; rather, they are committed to help others and surrender to a higher power. As the meaning of addiction is subject to meditated interpretation through testimonial meetings and as the respective steps are completed and exercised, the process of spiritual transformation induces the construction of a new flourishing identity. Almost all participants declared that they experienced spiritual and personal changes perceptibly recognizable by their friends and family members.

> I apply the NA principles in our life. I'm trying to keep my principles without talking openly about them. If my child is making a mistake right now, he has to explain his mistake. If I'm listening well, then I find out that he has learned from me. I practice this every day by accepting my mistakes and being honest with myself and others. I let my child learn from his mistakes and accept them. I practice the principles to try to incorporate them in my life without reminding people about them. If I do not practice them, I am forced to pretend to follow them without actually practicing them. I entered the society while those principles were part of me. (Male participant, eighteen years in NA)

The lifestyle of people who use substances is a combination of poverty, unemployment, and homelessness that occasionally rationalizes the perpetration of crimes to fund their clandestine habits. As one of the participants explained, "I sold everything of value and asked my family and friends to give me money." Yet once they join NA and start practicing the twelve steps, many stop engaging in criminal activities.

> My husband and I spent all of our money, and he also lost his job. All our deposits went to drugs. We asked for money from our parents, friends, and relatives. Nobody trusts us anymore to give us money. We started to sell everything from our home, whatever you can think of. We were left with one heater in our home. I wanted to go to the street and sell my child or start prostituting to obtain drugs. My husband started to steal mobile phones from his friend's store. (Female participant, nine years in NA)

There were several opportunities when I could steal something. I did, but my feeling after that was so bad. My viewpoint in NA has been changed completely. Because NA increased my awareness, now I know that stealing money does not solve my problems. (Female participant, nine years in NA)

According to the interlocutors, polyamorous relationships are common among people who use drugs. Women who use substances often trade sex for drugs; however, finding a partner who can financially support their habit is often challenging and they may find themselves trapped in undesirable sexual relationships with drug dealers. Most participants were raised in a dysfunctional family setting where they struggled with poverty from birth. Single women who use substances were mostly unemployed and escaped from home, and are left with no availing financial alternatives but to trade their bodies for drugs. In other cases, married women were dependent on their husbands, who also used substances, to obtain drugs; in rare cases, they abandoned their husband and found a partner who could support their addiction lifestyle. Although men who use substances also have polysexual relationships, financial issues were usually not the trigger. As NA fellows state, it is common for newcomers during the early stages of recovery to become involved in sexual relationships as a substitute for drugs. However, they advise not to get involved in sexual relationships with new partners and to stop promiscuous relationships with previous partners to focus on the recovery process. In other words, sexual relationships are one dimension of the addiction subculture, and maintaining sobriety is closely connected with managing sexual relationships; concentrating on the principles and collective goals is the most integral task of NA members.

I had a partner before I came to NA meetings. I started working on the steps in NA, and I chose someone as my sponsor. My sponsor told me that you must avoid your boyfriend because he is an addict, and you have a sexual dependency on him. She was right, as I did not quit drugs, but I still had my relationship with him. I had a sexual dependency, as sex was a good replacement for drugs for me. But the thing that really mattered at that period was working on the steps and practicing the steps with my sponsor. I had to attend the meetings every day and even twice a day. The reason was that the priority is to keep my connections with the recovering addicts to stay clean. One day, my boyfriend told me, "Why do you want to go to the meeting? Just forget it and come to my home." I told him that I cannot, and he said, "Please introduce some of your friends to me to and come to my home because I'm so alone." At that time, I realized I'm considered trash by him, and the only thing we had was sexual dependency. No more. He depressed me a lot. I broke up with him and concentrated on the steps. It worked. After 15 of years being a member of NA, I realized that all recovering addicts, specifically the single ones, must stop seeing their partners or not start any new relations. They must understand that all their relations in the very first months in NA just end up as sexual dependency relationships. It is just a distraction. They have to focus on their mission and take it seriously. (Female participant, twelve years of sobriety)

I really want to have an emotional relationship with someone, as I'm just 22 years old. My sponsor insists on preventing me from getting involved in any emotional relations with men. She tells me that I am not ready to have relationships with men. She tells me that I must work on the steps for at least one year, and then I might be ready. I know that I must focus on my treatment first, so I cut all my unmanageable sexual relations from the past. I live according to the specific principles and traditions of NA. I have specific criteria I use for choosing the people around me. My sponsor tells me that if you experience a failed emotional relationship before fully working on the steps and before being ready, the possibility of relapse is high. Then the steps do not work at all. (Female participant, eight months of sobriety)

The atmosphere at NA meetings must be protected from any inappropriate behavior which can make newcomers (especially those acutely suffering from addiction) feel uncomfortable, unwelcomed, excluded, ashamed, harassed, or scared. Novice NA members are the most vulnerable members in the respective meetings. They crave affection and acceptance. Thus, any violent behavior, such as verbal abuse, aggressive and threatening gestures, and physical violence is wholly discouraged and disallowed. Aggressive behaviors are most common among members who are still suffering addiction; meanwhile, experienced members are trained to educate and encourage them to participate in meetings without inappropriate behavior.

> In a situation of fighting or any kind of physical or verbal violence, there are two or three experienced recovering addicts with long lengths of clean time who will try to solve the problem. They know that once someone comes to NA for the first time, in the very first days, they act like a child; they cry and are very sensitive. They start to deal with realities. They remember divorcing their wife and losing their children, friends, and family members. Thus, they may act violently and aggressively; however, the recovering addicts invite them to calmness, talk to them, and encourage them to use dialogue instead of fighting. (Female participant, nine years in NA)

Constantly sharing testimonies with family members, in hope of their forgiveness, is a performance where people who have used substances present their new identity to create an opportunity to reform social and emotional bonds with their family. The process of testimony for drug-free citizens, in contrast to the NA members, is often limited to terse conversations. Most often, the process of stigmatization, exclusion, and marginalization prevents those in recovery from testifying among family members who were the primary group that caused the grounds for isolation. People who use substances, especially women, suffer from the stigma, blame, and labels that their families project onto them, as drug addiction is a traumatic and daunting familial issue. On the one hand, family members must deal with someone who is perceived as always looking to get high; on the other, they must seek to recuperate the perceived loss in family honor due to the violation of social and cultural norms by their loved ones who use substances. The notion of honor is a perennial concept sewed into the sociocultural fabric of society; it relates to others' opinions about the individuals (Oleinik 2016). The importance

102　Life on Drugs in Iran

of honor culture in some societies possesses such lofty valence that it is considered an expression or correlate of human dignity. People who use substances often abandon their home and, through their absence, the family has a chance to reform and rebuild the familial structure and revitalize lost honor. In some cases, people who use drugs do not leave their family which often induces more dysfunctional behaviors among the members. Once people who use substances attend the NA twelve-step recovery program, they have a chance to restore their relationships with family members. The process of treatment and recovery in NA requires members to rebuild relationships with their spouses, parents, and children.

> I compensate indirectly by calling my family, buying something for them, and dropping by to say hello. To compensate, I start communication and dialogue with neighbours in our community to announce that I'm not addicted anymore. (Male participant, five years of sobriety)

Working the twelve steps is analogous to burying the seeds for spiritual growth and maturity, honesty, acceptance, open-mindedness, and faith in a higher power. Believing in a higher power restores members' sanity and provides hope for recovery. Through the second step (i.e., we came to believe that a power greater than ourselves could restore us to sanity), NA members begin to believe that there is an indomitable power that guides them through the path of healing. This step requires working on open-mindedness to accept the greater power capable of healing and to confer trust toward the greater power as a companion during recovery, and a willingness to restore sanity.

> I did not believe in God at all. When I entered the program, I denied the existence of the greater power or God or whatever. But I remember that all the long-termers just smiled at me and gave me hope. They told me that whatever you believe in, just stay here and keep coming back. After a while and working on the steps, I began to believe in miracles. I believed that something greater than me saved me and protected me. God helped me through this painful passage. (Female participant, eight years in NA)

Gender-Based Reintegration

Multiple Powerlessness

Women who use substances are perceived as violating social norms and taboos concerning motherhood with perceived sexual promiscuity, regardless of the latency in veracity of the respective judgements. The inevitable component of stigmatization toward women who use substances is related to casual sex which is perceived as a threat to the honor of family, community, and society, and to the primary role of women—motherhood. Moreover, survivors of familial rape are subjected to even more brutal stigmas as they are perceived as infected and polluted in addition to being a criminal (Malloch 2011). The inevitable phenomenon of exclusion and powerlessness of women who use substances is metaphorically like the "Shaking Minaret." The Shaking Minaret is a historical monument located in Isfahan, Iran, comprised of two circular brick towers. When one of the towers shakes by human force, the other will shake simultaneously. In the case of women, drug dependence per se would be adequate to shake multiple stigmas. As noted earlier, this perception is not confined to the views of drug-free citizens in society, but also of their male counterparts in NA. One NA long-term member, who oversaw provisioning venues for women's NA meetings, was assaulted by the owner of a venue after learning about the reason behind renting the location.

> One day, I went to an institution to ask for an available place to hold NA meetings for women. A man who was in charge of that department asked me if there are any addict women. I was totally embarrassed in front of the others, and then he said that if there are any addict women, there is a stable outside of the city, and you can hold the meeting there. That was so embarrassing. Once he found out that the women's NA meeting will be held there, he started to directly underestimate them and even pretended that there are no addict women. (Female participant, twelve years in NA)

The powerlessness of women is intensified by full dependency on male partners to fund their habits. Kohn (1992) states that the nature of drug addiction is unfeminine because it is followed by sexual enslavement and illicit drug use, which clearly is not commensurate with female independence. In the current study, all female participants declared that their dependency on drugs pushed them toward being more dependent on men—drug suppliers are usually men, and the drug network is governed by men. Drugs and poverty often push women to sell sex, and men who possess drugs often leverage women's drug addictions as a means toward sexual exploitation. While for women, financial needs have been a strong motivation for having multiple sexual partners, sexual satisfaction and pleasure played a significant role in men's choice. Nevertheless, women who use substances are condemned for unrestricted sexuality and are suspected of maintaining the habit, even after achieving sobriety in NA. Men in recovery are exempt from this sexual stigmatization. As Morrissey (1986, 159) states, "All examination of how we define and discuss a problem or fail to address it is essentially an examination of relations of power." When women who use drugs are provided illicit substances by their husbands, these women tend not to engage in polyamory, albeit they are inevitably labeled as sex workers. This is despite the considerable difference when compared to women who were coerced into polyamorous relationships. Women who were provided substances by their husbands do not experience emotional and sexual harassment during addiction, but the memories remain painful.

> The only thing that I am thankful about is my husband, who provided drugs for me for ten years and did not let me have any contact with the drug dealers. At least I was just one who used substances, not an addict woman who sold my body for drugs. The harms that single addict women experience take years and years to heal due to having unwanted relations with drug dealers. (Female participant, ten years in NA)

In contrast, some women who use substances abandon their husbands or partners and become directly involved in drug networks. Exposure to the drug trade and its perpetrators make these women highly vulnerable.

> I did not have money, so I called the drug dealer, and he told me, "If you want drugs, you have to have sex with me." That was shameful because

the drug dealer was the same age as my boy. He was just 19 years old, but at that time, it did not matter to me. I had sex with him, and he did not give me drugs. I did not know how to describe this story in front of others in NA meetings. I had sexual relations with another drug dealer while I lived with my husband. I asked the drug dealer to come to my home, and I gave him a room. My husband witnessed everything in the home, but he did not say anything to anybody. We threatened him, and we forced him to use drugs to shut his mouth. My husband was always begging me for drugs, and I provided his drugs to keep him needy. I did not tell anybody about my secret partner at my home. My boy was there, at home. He saw everything. I did not even cook for him. One day, I locked him in the room for the whole day, and at the end of the day, I remembered that he was still locked in without anything to eat or drink. (Female participant, thirteen years in NA)

Men who use substances discussed similar stories, having engaged in polyamorous relations. They abandoned their family, refused to pay alimony or child support, and sometimes tortured family members physically and psychologically. However, these are not perceived as a violation of traditional gender roles; their behaviors are not considered morally wrong, and they are not condemned as poor fathers. Women who use substances on the other hand are criticized as being poor parents or unfeminine and are commonly derided with vulgar vituperation (e.g., whore). They are perceived as not knowing how to raise their children, serve their husbands, or care for their own well-being and personal appearance. In other words, they are perceived as violating all moral, social, and cultural codes in the name of drugs.

In families with parents who use substances, even children refer to their mothers as "useless whores." While they exclude their mothers from their lives, fathers who use substances continue to live with them. This reveals the multivariate complexity of the addiction phenomenon for women.

According to Williams (1998), women who use substances are doubly deviant, as they engage in illegal activity and violate feminine roles (i.e., raising children, pregnancy, breastfeeding). Their dependence on drugs causes them to be considered more deviant than men, especially when the user is the mother of a child and her ability to be a good mother is negated (Taylor 1993). Female participants repeatedly mentioned feeling that because they neglected their children, their children are the silent victims of their dependency. They are not just confined by bars, walls, and deprivation of institutions, but also by the fear, loneliness, hopelessness, and doubt which are most often associated with their children's circumstances and their lost societal honor.

Women experience multiple forms of powerlessness (e.g., being perceived as an addict, a criminal, a poor mother, and a prostitute), making the process of rehabilitation more complicated than for men. The same course of actions is practiced in NA, which is a representative of equality and purports that "all of us are the same." People who use substances suffer from different forms of powerlessness when attending their first NA meeting; for most men, the processes of empowerment and rehabilitation take hold more quickly.

> Men in NA have a much stronger belief in themselves than women. They are given much more power and hope from society. When addict men came to the NA program, they did not lose their dignity and confidence, because despite all the exclusion and isolation they experienced, they never lived like addict women. Addict women were excluded everywhere and were trapped in undesirable sexual relations with different drug dealers. (Female participant, three years in NA)

NA women believe that some men in recovery do not collaborate with their women counterparts in their treatment and rehabilitation journey, indicating that the stereotypes attached to women and addiction have infiltrated the NA community. Additionally, they believe that women in recovery were sex workers who continue to seek romantic and sexual relationships which will only serve as distractions to all NA members. However, these misperceptions are gradually addressed or in some cases ignored by women through practicing the NA principles.

> I do not care what they are thinking, I wanted to be engaged in all social activities. They always blamed my husband who is also a NA member

that why you let your woman involve in public activities of NA. I stood up and fight. They still scared that they will be seduced by women, I don't care, it is their problem not mine. They think that our activities in public might ruin the reputation of NA. Who cares? I have even encouraged my sponsees to be involved in all activities. We dressed up very decently, we wear makeup and attend all meetings and activities whether they desire or not. (Female participant, nine years in NA)

Although women in recovery attempt to gain acceptance and alleviate their shame and fear through the NA program, they are judged by unspoken and furtive standards, even in the NA program. Both women in recovery and those who still use substances suffer the same pains in nature, but in different social contexts. In other words, NA subculture is not exempt from the multiple standards that women suffer in society. In society, women must deal with incarceration and the stigma of violating social and cultural expectations. This process of degradation and dehumanization continues within treatment programs, preventing many women from participating in public NA activities and services. Even if NA women demonstrate a willingness to take part, their male counterparts prefer to have as little contact as feasible with them. If NA women take on responsibilities in public services, which are mostly occupied by men, they are under the strict control and surveillance of their male counterparts. Any violation of arbitrary male expectations is considered sufficient justification to request the woman to resign.

Most recovering women do not have the tendency to join any public activities and services. Their fear of being stigmatized by the men in the NA program pushes them back. I decided to become a public servant, but my behaviors were under the severe control of recovering men. I know if I do something against their wishes, I will be asked to resign immediately. For example, if I have any secret relationships with one of the men in the program and they learn about that, they would ask me to resign. However, they would not ask the man to resign. It is so tricky to accompany recovering men in an NA program. You expect them to accept you as a recovering addict woman exactly the same as themselves, but the fact is that they do not consider us the same as themselves. We all

108   Life on Drugs in Iran

were addicts, but their perception is the same as all people in the society, and they consider us as someone who had different sexual relationships. (Female participant, eight years in NA)

Women are inundated by the layers of stigmatization, all of which make them reluctant to join the NA treatment program. Although the NA program is available to all people who suffer from substance use, regardless of their gender, women are exposed to stigmatization throughout their recovery journey that is mostly cast from men in recovery and from the women's families.

> You cannot believe that after being in NA for 15 years, my mother still called me a whore. Whenever the style of my dress was against her will, she referred to me as a whore and a bitch. I remember the first 8 years of being in NA, my boy, who was 15 years old, yelled at me at home and called me a whore. This was not restricted to my family members, as even in NA, for the first years, I could not explain the whole story of my life. I was too scared of being labelled or blamed again. Even some of the recovering addict men cannot accept us because they believe that we were whores. Being a whore and being sexually active is considered worse [by] men than being an addict. (Female participant, fifteen years in NA)

Women who use substances frequently experience trepidation in disclosing their sufferings in the hope of receiving support, which inevitably leads toward emotional distress. As a result, they are less likely to reach out to treatment programs. Even if they could be a member of NA, it is challenging for them to share their addiction history, suffering, distress, and needs. Women who use substances must get through various social and cultural barriers to participate in NA meetings. Their families discourage and, in some cases, prevent them from attending any treatment programs; NA meetings are not an exception.

> Most recovering NA women abandon the NA meetings and their friends in NA once they get clean. In fact, they are afraid of being known in public or losing their anonymity. They are afraid of their family members. (Female participant, ten years in NA)

Stretching Normality

Family Support

The importance of the family's role in the treatment process is noteworthy. Reintegration into the family and restoring relationships with loved ones appear less challenging and comparatively more expeditious for men in recovery.

> My mother just sent me some money in prison irregularly, but she did not trust me. She sent money after I called her ten thousand times. She knew that I needed money to buy drugs in prison. She knew I did not spend this money on clothes or food. I threatened, shouted, cursed her, and pretended that I needed money for food. After I came to the recovery camp and stayed clean for more than 6 months, she spoke to me and she sent me money and clothes. She is beginning to trust me. (Male participant, ten years in NA)

However, women are deprived of the familial support system. The process of reintegration into one's family and society is demanding for women; in some cases, it is impossible. One of the most important indicators of being included and considered as part of society for people in recovery is restoring and reconstructing attachments to family. While women are blamed for being a careless and neglectful mother or wife, they do not receive any assistance from their family to rebuild their emotional and social ties. These conflicting strategies are impacted by the contradictory policies and laws of the state and how its social orders are imposed on the entire population. One of the most important accelerators in the recovery process is a reduction in the exclusions imposed by family members. In a few cases, the process of eliminating and eradicating stigma in the family occurred smoothly, contiguously with the efforts of the person in recovery to repair their dysfunctional behaviors and work toward the path of healing.

> My mother used to assault me and consider me as an embarrassment of the family, but now she can't stand even when I go on a short journey. She loves me now. (Female participant, ten years in NA)

110   Life on Drugs in Iran

However, some women in recovery declared that after five or even fifteen years of sobriety and countless attempts to heal their relationships with family members, they are still labeled as a whore. Although their family members might believe they are no longer fettered to substance use, they are still considered polyamorous. Despite all their efforts to make peace with their addiction history, women in recovery are perceived by their family as deviants. Socio-cultural barriers persistently push them back to their previous life; their history continues to define and haunt their present life.

> My family members, especially my son and my husband, are so sensitive about NA. My husband is an addict, and when I come home from NA meetings, he starts questioning about why I am hanging out with recovering addict women. He tells me that I am jeopardizing the dignity and honor of the family. In fact, my husband is not worried about me starting to use drugs; rather, he is worried about his honor. They are scared about people in the society who might figure out my past. They might find out that I was an addict in the past, and my family might lose its honor. They tell me that my sponsees are all physically embarrassing because they use drugs. Thus, whenever people see me around them, they will judge me or think I am an addict, too. Nobody is worried about me and my health; they all worry that they might lose their honor. (Female participant, four years in NA)

5

Contested Identity in Prison and Rehabilitation

The Challenge of Living with a Contested Identity

Despite the socio-structural differences between NA and prison, contested identities are common in both contexts. Whether it occurs under the banner of criminalization or disguised medicalization, the state employs control and monitoring over people who use substances through acknowledging them as a so-called dangerous and deviant class. Contradictory policies (i.e., securitization and treatment-oriented approaches) effactually subject the identities of people who use substance to constant manipulation. Contested perceptions of the state and society penetrate the lives of people in recovery, never allowing them to articulate a united, non-predetermined identity. This is exemplified in the case for NA women. In other words, overall unity between contested identities may not be possible; the contradictory policies of the state allow few opportunities for people who use or have used substances to decrease the conflict they experience among their multiple selves. People who use substances struggle with multiple, fluid, contested, and hybrid identities, regardless of the context (i.e., prison or treatment centers).

Contested Identity and Prison

The current study reveals that the prisons designated for drug-related criminals (i.e., compulsory labor camps) are characterized by high rates of violence and prevalence of drugs. People who use substances are arrested

111

112   Life on Drugs in Iran

and incarcerated in institutions governed and controlled by drug networks, and most participants were dismayed by their sentences in compulsory labor camps. Demarcating between people who use substances but are not major drug traffickers and the rest of the prison population necessarily implies the negation of the objective of establishing separate compulsory labor camps. While the objective is supposedly geared towards the decriminalization of people who use substances, they are treated as criminals and are inescapably surrounded by drugs.

> If you are lucky, you will be locked up in the prison, but God help you if you end up serving in the compulsory labor camps. It is like a cemetery. People are dying in the camps every day. They are killed in fights or conflicts over drugs, or they die from drug overdoses. The high rate of death due to drug overdoses is a major phenomenon in the camps. You just feel confused as to why they arrested and locked us up here. We can find drugs much easier in the camps and smoke as much as we want, so what is the point? I don't understand whether I am a criminal or just one who uses substances. I wish they had sent me to the real prison. This is a jungle. (Male participant, nine years of incarceration)

Methadone Maintenance Treatment (MMT) and NA are two examples of medicalization approaches in prisons. However, their functions have been overshadowed by the dominant criminalization approach. After incarceration, people who use substances are surrounded by drugs in a more logistically refined environment than in society. Drug trafficking in prison is a highly profitable business, as it can cover all expenses of the incarcerated prisoner's life and the needs of their family members on the other side of the wall. In the name of promoting health and safety, especially for those who inject heroin, MMT has become a complementary methodology in prisons. Despite the performative showcase of law amendments, transformations, and movements from criminalization to medicalization along with an emphasis on MMT, drugs are regularly smuggled into the prison with guards' assistance. The widespread availability of drugs, with no fear of apprehension by anti-narcotic enforcement, and furthermore being encouraged to register for MMT, eradicates any chance of the development of a unified identity among people who use substances.

I don't know what to choose, but thank God there are lots of way to be intoxicated in prison, from methadone to heroin. On one hand, we are encouraged or forced to use methadone in the prison, while on the other hand you witness people who inject heroin in the bathrooms. I end up using both. It is like a joke, but not a funny one. You get your daily dose of methadone, and right after that you buy heroin to inject. It is unbelievable. We are all a target of the state to make money. Believe me or not, most of those drugs have been smuggled by the guards or by prisoners who bribe the guards well. Now, in this situation I don't know what kind of drugs I'm using and why I do so. I don't know whether methadone is better or heroin. I play in front of those who are just using methadone and pretend that I'm one of them, but one minute later you can find me among heroin injectors in the bathroom. This is our life; we don't know who we are. If they let us alone, the chance that we would find out by ourselves is higher than with their stupid interventions. (Male participant, nine years of incarceration)

Although NA has been operating in Iranian prisons, neither those who use substances nor prison guards believe in its function in the penal system. For example, guards explicitly, even sarcastically, refer to NA as a hobby in prison. The number of NA followers in prisons is not comparable with those who use MMT either as a treatment or complementary option. The dominance of securitization over the treatment approach regarding addiction and people who use substances is obvious in prison. Those who are true followers of the twelve-step NA program in prison struggle with inner contested identities in a prison system where criminalization is practiced by guards and prisoners. The implicit conflict between contradictory policies and programs leaves inmates in limbo. This blurred line has enforced the necessity of playing contrasting roles and employing contrasting lenses. They must adopt multiple identities and roles to act in accordance with various situations. To avert trouble in prison where the dominance of criminalization and punishment is prevalent, the inmates must maintain an appearance of toughness, aggressiveness, and hypermasculinity so they do not appear weak or subservient among other inmates. However, they internalize another contrasting persona, involving an expression of vulnerability and powerlessness.

114   Life on Drugs in Iran

> Our identity is like a frozen stone that has been hit by a huge hammer and broken into a hundred pieces. Being an NA member in prison is like that. When I step out of the meetings, the cruel fight starts between you and the system. Even the guards don't believe in NA, and it takes lots of energy to convince them you have changed. It does not matter that the NA program is in prison, as they don't believe in these kinds of treatment. They still believe in punishments. You know even the methadone is not operated to help or cure us. It is just for controlling us. Managing us. It works much faster than any other solution. Even prisoners, almost all of whom are addicts, don't believe anything will work for them, let alone NA. They even make fun of methadone, as it is like candy for them. (Male participant, six years of incarceration)

Incarcerated women who serve their sentences with their children often are forced into sobriety immediately after their arrest. The detoxification process occurs without preliminary equipment or knowledge, and they are left alone in the mother-child ward for several days until the detoxification process is complete. On some occasions, cellmates provide the mother with painkillers surreptitiously. After an arbitrary detoxification, the woman resumes her struggles with multiple defeated identities as a mother, wife, daughter, and/or grandmother while maintaining her motherhood identity to serve her child in prison. They bear the burden of permanent feelings of guilt and shame from the perception that they are criminals and that their children have been affected by their actions. According to Agamben, the survivors of the camp are innocent, but they are obliged to feel guilty; they are "guilty-innocent" people (Agamben 1998, 94). "In shame, the subject has no content other than its own desubjectification; it becomes witness to its own disorder" (Agamben 1998, 106). They are classified as inhuman or *musellmann*; women who use substances are like "staggering corpses" or "living dead," excluded from family and society without compassion.

> I was left alone on the floor, next to the front door, in the mother-child ward. I was not even provided with a blanket. One of the mothers covered me with an old blanket. My daughter was around all day, and I could not

Contested Identity in Prison and Rehabilitation   115

move because of unbearable pain all over my body. When I recovered, I again started to fight against a different "me." I'm a criminal, whatever I do, and the society knows me as a criminal. I was an addict for years, and during all that time, I tried to quit, but I could not, and one of the reasons was not having any emotional support. Nobody from the society or my family considered me as a patient. I needed to be cured, but nobody helped, as they called me a criminal and a prostitute instead. It was the same story in prison. I was clean and tried to be a mother, but I still struggled with the idea of whether I am a mother or criminal. Can I be a good mother with an addiction history? I always have to fight with myself. (Female participant, three years of incarceration)

Prisoners are struggling with dynamic and fluid identities; however, this is not the case for major drug traffickers who are mostly gang leaders. The lack of privacy in prison has been recognized as a functional prerequisite of incarceration (Schwartz 1971, 229) and it is also considered part of the pain of imprisonment (Sykes 1958). Furthermore, since prison security is achieved through several mechanisms and forms of surveillance over inmates, there is no reasonable expectation of privacy in prison due to the required transparency of the environment. According to Oleinik (2017, 55), "The transparency of the public/private border makes surveillance easy and omnipresent: both the penal authorities and all of the inmates are committed to it." However, in Iranian prisons, the hierarchy determines the scope of private territory for each inmate. High-status positions have private space in public which is proportionate to their life outside of prison. By privacy, it is meant that the space is closed off to others who might wish to share it. The space is even untouchable by prison guards and correctional officers, since almost all inmates with high-status positions have close relationships based on mutual benefits with the guards. Sometimes the private space is determined by a cell door, but most often a single curtain defines the kinship territory. This privacy provides an opportunity for a limited number of prisoners to express their arbitrary identity with less instability and contradiction by applying dominance over the local territory. However, subordinate prisoners are exposed to instantaneous changes, which results in wearing a "mask" and constantly falling in line with perpetually changing rules. Although all prisoners who use substances are to some extent affected by contested identities in prison, inmates far from the source of power (i.e., far from high status criminals) are the most affected, while inmates in the intermediate and peak layers of the hierarchy are protected by power which decreases the challenges associated with identity configuration.

Contested identity and NA

Despite the growing number of treatment centers, from harm reduction to treatment and recovery centers, it is noteworthy that people who use substances are still highly criminalized. Joining the NA community and practicing NA principles does not immediately trigger an identity transformation toward normalcy. This is an elusive goal even under the banner of pseudo-medicalization. Restricted trust toward drug-free citizens and a lack of sense of belonging to society yield multiple identities.

> I cannot communicate with people in the society whether my family and friends or strangers the same way that I'm communicating with my NA fellows. It is not possible. They called me for many years criminal, junkie, and addict. They did not recruit me. They did not trust me. They left me. Now you expect me to behave with them the same way. No NA fellows are like me, all of them. We have never left each other behind. We support each other. Me with NA fellow is different from me with the non-NA members. (Male participant, eight years in NA)

The dominance of the criminalization approach penetrates the life of people who use substances to the extent that they face considerable resistance when attempting to attend medication-assisted treatment programs. The constant feelings of failure and rejection by society and particularly family members reinforce their contested identity. Even if women who use substances desire to achieve sobriety, the fear of being stigmatized acts as a deterrent which dissuades them from seeking treatment. The extensive stigmatization and exclusion due to addiction, pursuing sexual relations, and not meeting the expectations of motherhood exacerbate the challenges women experience with respect to seeking treatment. Although

Contested Identity in Prison and Rehabilitation   117

people who use substances, regardless of their gender, are considered criminal and do not fit under the category of ordinary citizens, the reintegration of males in recovery into society is comparatively less challenging. Women who use substances break social norms and gender roles; thus, they are simply understood as anomalies and fundamentally this makes the reintegration process much more onerous. Even some male NA members stigmatize their female counterparts, disparagingly referring to them as "toys in the hands of drug dealers."

> Yes, I completely agree that being an addict is no different than being a criminal. I know because I live with this perception. But the thing is that the social pressures over men are not comparable with ours. I am always stuck among different kinds of me. I always struggle with being an NA member, addict, criminal, bad mother, not a decent woman. (Female participant, fifteen years in NA)

The criminalization elements in NA's subculture affect the process of recovery among women. Although criminalization has caused people who use substances to suffer stigma to some extent, in the male-dominated Iranian society, male power acts as a veil in the perennial process of "double consciousness." The gradual process of internalizing the negative perceptions of mainstream society towards females in recovery provides fertile soil for the double consciousness phenomenon. According to W. E. B. DuBois (1903, 3), double consciousness is a "sense of always looking at one's self through the eyes of others, of measuring one's soul by the tape of a world that looks on in amused contempt and pity."

> No, it is an endless effort for NA women. Maybe we are just considered as "patients" among other NA fellows, but not among men or in the society. We have a different life, one with our NA fellows and one with the rest of people in the society, including NA men. (Female participant, nine years in NA)

The NA community provides an opportunity for both women and men in recovery to be in constant contact with drug-free citizens through public meetings and compensation to restore their relationships and to reintegrate into society. One of the most important effects of NA, as a nongovernmental organization, is the migration of identities across different social contexts. The mass identity migration and transformation simultaneously among three different social contexts (i.e., the addiction context, NA context, and society context) make the boundaries disappear. The interaction between the varying social orders of different contexts in limited time and space can be rendered possible in NA meetings (in particular, public meetings). Considering the identity of NA members as a reflexive project reveals that the addiction identity loses its dominant power and in return, NA gives the opportunity for members to continually examine, shape, monitor, and reform their identity in the light of NA principles, addiction life experiences, and the socially desirable and acceptable identity.

Some NA members believe that even if they are part of the NA community, which is a home for fellowship, their identities jump in and out of different social contexts across different time periods. The addiction, according to NA principles, continually haunts those in recovery, even if they are long-term NA members living drug-free lives.

The aggregate identity of people in recovery is representative of three different identities at the same time, which can be called the process of the construction and deconstruction of one's identity in NA. Although there is a constant clash between different identities in NA, a new identity is continually engaged in the process of emergence according to NA principles. However, it is not possible to isolate the recovery identity from other identities. On the one hand, the fluidity of an identity among different social contexts facilitates the treatment process through breaking the boundaries between those in recovery and the drug-free citizens in society. On the other, drug-free citizens become familiar with NA fellows' lifestyle and how they are rehabilitated through the NA principles to become active and productive members of society. Social perceptions regarding addiction differ over time and are reformed by various forces, which reveal that there is no static or fixed line or boundary between the "in crowd" and "out crowd" in society (Sanders 2014). Rather, the process of stigmatization and exclusion of people who use substances are socially constructed

Contested Identity in Prison and Rehabilitation   119

and reconstructed, which might be further influenced through the passage of time.

The reality of identity transformation is that NA members adapt to a new set of social orders which are added to their previous identities. The previous identities become colorless, while the new one is vitalized. The continuing project of constructing and reconstructing an identity vividly presents the negotiation between the previous, current, and possible identities. Testimony or narrative is the principal component of the identity formation and reformation process. Testimony is not the process of awakening or restoring the old identity or normal identity (i.e., before addiction); rather, it is the process of reinterpreting, reconstructing, and redefining all the multiple engaged identities to decrease the inherent conflict. The process of interpreting multiple identities, from addiction, criminality, and prostitution to the gender-expected roles, assists them to reinterpret various elements of their identities to construct a clarified image of them. The process of telling stories and narratives to those who are considered "us" and not "them" mitigates the intensity of the inner conflict. However, a contested identity is a continuing project in the lives of NA members, especially women.

Although a contested identity is an inseparable component of their life, whether in prison or NA, the agency of those in recovery through the NA program cannot be overlooked. Some NA members, regardless of their gender, mitigate inner identity struggles by participating in NA meetings, being active in NA events and services, restoring their relationships with family, continuing their education, searching for a vocation, and overcoming their fears and shame. Those who end up in the NA community despite endless struggles with contested identities are at least lucky enough to be trained and to have the opportunity to learn the necessary social skills required to accelerate their reintegration into society. Almost all interviewees stated that although it is quite impossible for NA members to resume normal life, the chance of being considered a productive part of society can be increased by practicing NA principles. Even if the NA subculture encouraged its fellows towards an "us" and "them" mentality, it provides a sense of belonging to a group which can in turn supply

120   Life on Drugs in Iran

the confidence needed to rebuild their lives by taking a less challenging path. Participants who joined NA and later disconnected from their fellow members declared that being in NA, regardless of all the disadvantages, makes the reintegration pathway more feasible. Those participants who abandoned NA meetings after achieving sobriety seem to have even more inner conflict than those who kept attending NA meetings. Thus, it can be said that NA meetings and the testimony process act analogous to a projector in an addiction warehouse, which makes the previous, current, and potential identities visible enough to analyze, while those who become disconnected with the NA program, as they mentioned, are being lost in their complex identities.

Ubiquity of Contested Identity

One of the most important components of life for people who use substances, either in prison or in NA, is the formation of contested or multiple identities which is a distinctive feature and an inescapable issue even in the modern era where a normal identity is plural and contested. In the modern era, one is "caught up in so many different, sometimes conflicting, roles that one no longer knows who one is" (Kellner 1992, 143). The salient point is that though individuals in today's society struggle with contested and fractured identities, this is still considered normal; however, this contrasts with addicts' identities, which are characterized by multiple exclusive identities.

According to Giddens (1990), identity in the modern world is a reflexive project which is no longer affected by traditions and locality and is not limited to the territory of a specific context or community. Rather, the formation and reformation of identity is entirely the responsibility of the individual. Or, as Wieviorka (2004, 290) states, "identities are chosen and adopted by the subjective decisions that are made by individuals." In fact, identities are not "the automatic outcome of reproduction, or a legacy from the past." Rather, "modernity means the permanent creation of the world by human beings who are endowed with the power and ability to create data and language" (Touraine 1995, 230).

Contested Identity in Prison and Rehabilitation   121

Although people with drug-free lifestyles to some extent also move across different identities and subsequently struggle with contested, conflicted, and multiple identities, unwanted individuals have a rare chance to extricate themselves and move away from the contiguous territories and boundaries of identities. Freedom of movement among different territories of identities belongs only to specific citizens, not to all of them. The territoriality of the so-called "dangerous" class is more subdued and controlled. Put another way, in the modern era, the identities of individuals freely travel across each other, even with clashes or conflicts; but the process is not the same for the excluded people in society. The identity mobility of people who use drugs is restricted to predefined identities (e.g., prostitute, addicted, and criminal). The transition from tradition to modernity pushes citizens toward being more reliant on their own actions instead of institutions, and people who use drugs experience the transition toward complexity in the most extreme and brutal form. Individuals have a greater chance to construct and reconstruct, form and reform, interpret and reinterpret their identities based on various types of information and social changes, while predefined and oppressive identities are forced upon the marginalized, abnormal, and unwanted people in society.

Even members of NA or any treatment center in Iran are fettered in a cycle of conflict that pushes them back and forth toward the most fragmented self; from the recovery identity and future potential identities to the addiction identity. As DuBois (1903) elaborates, marginalized and isolated individuals in society are less likely to experience the "unitary" self as an "essence." The only occasion where people who use drugs break the cycle of their dominant identities and step forward to exercise agency over their own identity occurs in NA; however, this does not happen for all individuals, especially women. Even by breaking the vicious cycle, the previously defined identities continue the process of conflict and struggle. Thus, I am not suggesting that the identity of people who use drugs is predetermined and that they no longer have agency; neither am I speaking of individuals in NA who become a subject in terms of freedom and act against the logic of power to construct social experiences as Touraine (1995) states. Rather, during the process of recovery in NA, the combination of determination and agency constructs the identity of NA members. According to Giddens (1990), human agency and structures are interconnected and interrelated with each other; even though social structures affect individual acts, they can be negotiated, restructured, and reproduced by social actions. In other words, "society only has form, and that form only has effects on people, in so far as structure is produced and reproduced in what people do" (Giddens and Pierson 1998, 77).

Although identity is defined by fluidity, plurality, and contestation in the modern world, people who use drugs experience the most brutal transition process to the plural and contested states through exclusion from the rest of society, thereby forcing them to remain manacled to unnecessary struggles and the restriction of their free will. It is not suggested that labeling people who use drugs as criminals or "sick" only precludes certain parts of society from normal living; rather, the problem runs deeper. By painting people who use drugs as an abnormal, criminal, and unwanted group through contradictory anti-narcotic laws and policies, the "others" are perceived and constructed which makes the reintegration process much more challenging. Reintegration into society where the identity of the "others" is created is considered threatening to the perception of ordinary citizens. In fact, the reciprocal relations between the social structure and social actions reinforce the notion of the "unwanted others."

Conclusion

Failed Medicalization

My aim throughout this book is to convey the lived experiences of people who use or have used substances under contradictory official discourses which tether them to the labels of delinquency and/or sickness. The disguise of the medical approach in Iran should not be perceived as a departure from the criminalization approach; law-enforcement agencies still actively prosecute people who use substances. The emergence of never-accomplished medicalization has expanded the milieu of punishment instead of limiting its scope. As Conrad and Schneider (1980, 142) state, "We are left with a hybrid criminal designation of addiction: opiate addiction is still criminalized, but addicts are deemed suitable for medical treatment." In the name of health and medicine, people who use substances have been isolated, degraded, stigmatized, excluded, and punished on the streets, within families, and in prison and treatment centers. Many considered the application of a medical approach toward addiction as a manifestation of humanitarian and scientific progress. I argue that therapeutic and punitive approaches in Iran have produced various substitute prisons for people who use or have used substances. As Conrad and Schneider (1980, 250) state, "Defining deviant behavior as a medical problem allows certain things to be done that could not otherwise be considered . . . this treatment can be a form of social control."

By introducing the pseudo-medicalization approach as a painkiller, attention is diverted from the social roots and causes of addiction and shifted toward the individual. The lack of experts in the fields of addiction, medical facilities, scientific methods, and comprehensive follow-up processes leads people who use substances to be trapped in a contested status either in prison as criminals or in treatment organizations as so-called patients. According to Singer (1992, 43), "Both criminality and disease are conceived as outlaws, invaders with secret ways, as well as forces of disorder. Both criminality and disease (and their postulated equivalence) are used to rationalize forms of power in the name of maintaining a healthier, that is, crime-free and disease-free, society. Both rationalise power as management."

We must not be misled by the apparent contradiction between the two discourses. Instead, the idea that both of them refer to a single seamless web seems more relevant. While medicalization expresses the same punitive theme, it does so through pseudo-medical institutions where medicine either disappears together with treatment and rehabilitation or is confined to MMT at best.

As Slosar (1978) states, the principal aims of nongovernmental centers in the field of addiction are assumed to be based on treatment and rehabilitation by encouraging volunteer work in the institution, establishing close relationships with members, and developing accepted social habits, emotional maturity, and the capacity to deal with everyday problems. In Haj and Hashemi's words (2015, 36) "On the personal revolutionary plan, they try to make a total change in people's lifestyles with the aid of fellows' support." People who use substances face two choices: to be considered a worthy individual who seeks treatment or to be considered a criminal and deviant. I believe that fundamentally the coercive approach will be applied in both situations regardless of an individual's choice.

It is not my intention to underestimate agency or the counter-voices of people who have a history of substance use as a member of NGOs such as NA, nor to deny the fact that NA meetings, despite being affected by a crime-oriented approach, contribute to challenging the philosophy of criminalization. NA functions through the tenets of the twelve-step philosophy and by alleviating the coercive approach towards addiction by equipping members with a humanitarian ideology that transcends the endless array of challenges. Nonetheless, it is worth mentioning that some sort of dislocation of dependency is occurring even in NA. Dependency is routinely redirected from substance use and methadone to peer support.

Conclusion   125

A new dependency developed within the NA community is not restricted to having the constant companionship, support, encouragement, and inspiration of NA members, but also to excessive sexual relationships, overeating, oversleeping, and smoking tobacco.

Also, some may assume that NA is an equalizer, a place where those with a history of substance use are labeled normal as they practice morally praiseworthy and acceptable behaviors. However, despite facilitating the use of the more morally acceptable appellation of illness for people who use substances, I argue that NA members remain social outcasts. They call people with drug-free lifestyles "ordinary." In my very first meeting with the members of NA, I was introduced as an "ordinary" person (*adam-e adi*), a term that stems from the widely accepted us-versus-them mentality among NA members.

This distinction between us and them occurs for two main reasons. The most apparent one is the fact that people who use substances are constantly considered to be sick criminals. It is difficult to ascertain that professional suspicion or medical labels (e.g., being viewed as a patient, or diseased) protects people who use or have used substances from punishment or stigma. It might be assumed that medicalization reduces stigmas and projects a more humanitarian discourse toward addiction in society. However, this is simply not the case. The boundary between denoting a person as an addict or a patient is blurred, as people who use or have used substances are suffering from the contested identity of the patient criminal. The shadow of criminalization penetrates the mind and body of people who use or have used substances and even pushes NA members away from the sense of belonging to society. This is not the only community where the respective group does not feel a sense of belonging. Being considered a criminal creates an intragroup us-versus-them mentality as well. Some members discreetly discussed their uneasy feelings toward the NA society itself, as they referred to NA members as untrustworthy individuals who cannot be relied upon outside of the ambit of NA.

The second reason is rooted in the most latent belief among NA members that "ordinary" citizens are inferior to NA members since they are not blessed and equipped with NA principles. NA is a hierarchy-free organization, where one member wields status equal to any other. Yet, being an

NA member, especially a long-term sponsor with hundreds of sponsees, leads to the display of a sense of superiority in which non-NA members are perceived as being incapable of understanding NA principles, whereas members consider themselves much more knowledgeable and experienced in resolving issues (e.g., family conflict) and praise themselves for accomplishing the task of surviving addiction. Although it is not traceable within the group, this prevalence of a feeling of superiority among NA members was one of the major sources of complaints from family and friends about NA members.

Conrad and Schneider (1980) consider several positive impacts that can be attributed to the medicalization approach: creating humanitarian and therapeutic methods rather than retributive or punitive methods; reassessment of the role of the sick which reduces stigma, guilt, and blame; portraying an optimistic therapeutic approach which mobilizes hope; offering treatment by a prestigious medical profession; and applying more flexible and efficient rather than judicial and penal means of social control. Although neither of the approaches toward criminalization nor medicalization in Iran provide the aforementioned advantages in full, the treatment-oriented approaches may be more efficient in some respects than the crime-oriented ones. Their implementation gave rise to a flourishing business nationwide.

Therefore, I prefer to avoid describing these contradictory policies toward addiction in Iran as the coexistence of two separate discourses: criminalization and medicalization. Security-oriented discourses of addiction in Iran have endured, and it is not my intention to deny the efforts of harm-reduction centers in Iran. On the contrary, my goal is to promote the idea that if punishment remains the dominant approach, we may only witness incremental changes. That does not imply that all recovery and treatment centers apply nonscientific and retrograde approaches. Rather, the existing positive tendencies do not suffice to underpin the movement from criminalization to medicalization. Treatment and recovery centers in the addiction field function more as judicial references and profit-driven firms that are characterized by the "lack [of] human resources, both technical experts and field workers without whom these

Conclusion   127

early harm-reduction initiatives will fail to reach the necessary minimum threshold for effectiveness" (Alizade et al. 2020; Ohiri et al., 2006, p. 435). As Mohammad Fellah, the DCHQ director, states, " . . . as far as I know, most drug treatment organizations' employees barely have more than a high school diploma . . . these labor/recovery/treatment camps do not differ from prisons. What has been done in the camps is what had been done in prisons. Employees with the lack of knowledge were in charge and managing the prisons. The same happens in the treatment centers" (cited by Madani 2011, 475). It is not difficult to believe participants who proclaimed that being incarcerated is a much-preferred alternative to being locked in camps (especially state-run compulsory camps).

It might be assumed that power in Iranian society is both disciplinary and sovereign in Foucauldian terms. I prefer to say that it is sovereign with elements of fabricated disciplinarity. Some might consider that the function of treatment centers and other total institutions in Iran is, as Foucault states, to discipline human bodies based on a specific regime, improve their conditions, or optimize their productivity. By fabricating the truth, those are no more than a performative spectacle. It is not my intention to discuss the Iranian state based on Foucault's notion of power. Still, it is worth mentioning that Foucault (2007, 107–8) believes that in reality one has a triangle, sovereignty-discipline-government, which has as its primary target the population and as its essential mechanism the apparatuses of security. In the case of Iran, it might be more accurate to say that sovereignty coexists with the illusion of discipline and government. Christensen (2011) and Ghiabi (2019) used different figures of speech such as contradictory, conflicting, paradox, and oxymoron to illustrate the politics of the Iranian state, particularly as they pertain to drug addiction. I prefer to use the terms disguise and illusion.

I purposefully do not mention the so-called medicalization in the last paragraph since the crime-oriented approach outweighs the drug policies and penetrates recovery/treatment programs. It might be assumed that addiction is no longer considered a form of moral corruption and moral deprivation and a threat to national security, and people who use substances are no longer considered enemies or criminals, but rather

128 Life on Drugs in Iran

"vulnerable" or "patients." This assumption would be acceptable if we merely focused on the existence of treatment, recovery, and harm reduction centers by taking them out of the general context. Unfortunately, this is not only scientifically unsound but also counterfactual to the current situation.

References

Index

References

Abrahamian, E. 1999. *Tortured Confessions: Prisons and Public Recantations in Modern Iran*. Berkeley and Los Angeles: Univ. of California Press.

Agamben, Giorgio. 1998. *HOMO SACER: Sovereign Power and Bare Life*. Stanford: Stanford Univ. Press.

Akers, Ronald L., Norman S. Hayner, and Werner Gruninger. 1977. "Prisonization in Five Countries—Type of Prison and Inmate Characteristics." *Criminology* 14, no. 4: 527–54.

Alam-Mehrjerdi, Zahra, Mohammad Abdollahi, Peter Higgs, and Kate Dolan. 2015. "Drug Use Treatment and Harm Reduction Programs in Iran: A Unique Model of Health in the Most Populated Persian Gulf Country." *Asian Journal of Psychiatry* 16: 78–83.

Alizade, Mahnaz, Yousef Abazari, Farah Torkaman, and Abdolhosein Kalantari. 2020. "Bare sakht-e etiad va ravand-e obj-e sazi motad dar dahehay-e pas as enghelab 57." *Journal of Masael-e ejtemayi Iran* 1: 177–201.

Anaraki, Nahid R. 2021. *Prison in Iran: A Known Unknown*. Charn, Switzerland: Palgrave Macmillan.

Anaraki, Nahid Rahimipour, and Dariush Boostani. 2014. "Mother-Child Interaction: A Qualitative Investigation of Imprisoned Mothers." *Quality & Quantity* 48, no. 5: 2447–61.

Arnkoff, Diane B. 1980. "Psychotherapy from the Perspective of Cognitive Theory." In *Psychotherapy Process: Current Issues and Future Directions*, edited by Michael J. Mahoney, 339–61. Boston, MA: Springer.

Bachman, Ronet, and Russell K. Schutt. 2013. *The Practice of Research in Criminology and Criminal Justice*. Los Angeles: Sage Publications, Inc.

Bandyopadhyay, Mahuya. 2006. "Competing Masculinities in a Prison." *Men and Masculinities* 9, no. 2: 186–203.

132   References

Banks, Cyndi. 2003. *Women in Prison: A Reference Handbook*. Santa Barbara, CA: ABC-CLIO.

Bauman, Zygmunt. 2013. *Wasted Lives: Modernity and Its Outcasts*. Oxford: Polity Press. First published in 2004 by Polity Press in association with Blackwell Publishing Ltd.

Bayat, Asef. 1997. *Street Politics: Poor People's Movements in Iran*. Columbia, NY: Columbia Univ. Press.

Beacroft, Melanie. 2004. "Bauman, Wasted Lives and the Eclipse of the Political." Retrieved from https://www.adelaide.edu.au/apsa/docs_papers/Others/Beaucroft.pdf.

Behrouzan, Orkideh. 2010. "An Epidemic of Meanings: HIV and AIDS in Iran and the Significance of History, Language and Gender." In The Fourth Wave: Violence, Gender, Culture & HIV in the 21st Century, edited by Jennifer F. Klot and Vinh-Kim Nguyen, 319–46. Paris: UNESCO.

Behrouzan, Orkideh, and Michael M. J. Fischer. 2014. "Behaves Like a Rooster and Cries Like a [Four Eyed] Canine: The Politics and Poetics of Depression and Psychiatry in Iran." In *Genocide and Mass Violence: Memory, Symptom, and Recovery*, edited by Devon E. Hinton and Alexander L. Hinton, 105–36. Cambridge: Cambridge Univ. Press.

Berk, Bernard B. 1966. "Organizational Goals and Inmate Organization." *American Journal of Sociology* 71, no. 5: 522–34.

Blakeney, Ronnie Frankel, and Charles David Blakeney. 2006. "Delinquency: A Quest for Moral and Spiritual Integrity." In *The Handbook of Spiritual Development in Childhood and Adolescence*, edited by Eugene C. Roehlkepartain, Pamela Ebstyne King, Linda M. Wagener, and Peter L. Benson, 371–83. Thousand Oaks, CA: Sage Publications, Inc.

Blomberg, Thomas G., and Karol Lucken. 2017. *American Penology: A History of Control*. Enl. 2nd ed. Oxfordshire, UK: Routledge.

Bowen, Glenn A. 2006. "Grounded Theory and Sensitizing Concepts." *International Journal of Qualitative Methods* 5, no. 3: 12–23.

Bowker, Lee H. 1981. "Gender Differences in Prisoner Subcultures." In *Women and Crime in America*, edited by Lee H. Bowker, 409–19. New York: Macmillan.

Boys, Annabel, Jane Fountain, J. Marsden, P. Griffiths, G. Stillwell, and J. Strang. 2000. *Drugs Decisions: A Qualitative Study of Young People*. London: Health Education Authority.

Britton, Dana M. 2003. *At Work in the Iron Cage*. New York: New York Univ. Press.

Brown, Scott C., R. A. Stevens, Peter F. Troiano, and Mary Kay Schneider. 2002. "Exploring Complex Phenomena: Grounded Theory in Student Affairs Research." *Journal of College Student Development* 43, no. 2: 173–83.

Bullock, Tony. 2003. "Changing Levels of Drug Use Before, During and After Imprisonment." In *Prisoners' Drug Use and Treatment: Seven Research Studies*, edited by M. Ramsey, 23–48. London: Home Office Research, Development and Statistics Directorate.

Cain, Maureen. 1990. "Towards Transgression: New Directions in Feminist Criminology." *International Journal of the Sociology of Law* 18, no. 1: 1–18.

Calabrese, John. 2007. "Iran's War on Drugs: Holding the Line." *The Middle East Institute, Policy Brief* 3: 1–18.

Camp, George M. 1985. *Prison Gangs: Their Extent, Nature, and Impact on Prisons*. Washington, DC: US Department of Justice, Office of Legal Policy, Federal Justice Research Program.

Camp, Scott D., Gerald G. Gaes, Neal P. Langan, and William G. Saylor. 2003. "The Influence of Prisons on Inmate Misconduct: A Multilevel Investigation." *Justice Quarterly* 20, no. 3: 501–33.

Charmaz, K. 2003. "Grounded Theory: Objectivist and Constructivist Methods." In *Strategies for Qualitative Inquiry*, edited by N. K. Denzin and Y. S. Lincoln, 249–91. Thousand Oaks, CA: Sage Publications, Inc.

Chenitz, W. Carole, and Janice M. Swanson. 1986. *From Practice to Grounded Theory: Qualitative Research in Nursing*. Boston: Addison-Wesley.

Cho, Ji Young, and Eun-Hee Lee. 2014. "Reducing Confusion About Grounded Theory and Qualitative Content Analysis: Similarities and Differences." *Qualitative Report* 19, no. 32: 1–20.

Christensen, Janne Bjerre. 2011. *Drugs, Deviancy and Democracy in Iran: The Interaction of State and Civil Society*. New York: Bloomsbury Publishing.

Christie, Nils. 2016. *Crime Control as Industry: Towards Gulags, Western Style*. London: Routledge.

Clark, Judith. 1995. "The Impact of the Prison Environment on Mothers." *Prison Journal* 75, no. 3: 306–29.

Clemmer, Donald. 1940. *The Prison Community*. New York: Holt, Rinehart and Winston.

Cline, Hugh Francis, and Stanton Wheeler. 1966. "The Determinants of Normative Patterns in Correctional Institutions." PhD diss., Harvard Univ.

Cloward, Richard A. 1960. "Social Control in the Prison." *Theoretical Studies in Social Organization of the Prison* 15: 20–48.

134   References

Connell, Robert W. 1998. "Masculinities and Globalization." *Men and Masculinities* 1, no. 1: 3–23.

Conrad, Peter. 1992. "Medicalization and Social Control." *Annual Review of Sociology* 18, no. 1: 209–32.

Conrad, Peter, and Joseph W. Schneider. 1980. *The Medicalization of Deviance: From Badness to Sickness*. St Louis, MO: Mosby.

Corbin, Juliet M., and Anselm Strauss. 1990. "Grounded Theory Research: Procedures, Canons, and Evaluative Criteria." *Qualitative Sociology* 13, no. 1: 3–21.

Corra, Mamadi, and David Willer. 2002. "The Gatekeeper." *Sociological Theory* 20, no. 2: 180–207.

Cox, Verne C., Paul B. Paulus, and Garvin McCain. 1984. "Prison Crowding Research: The Relevance for Prison Housing Standards and a General Approach Regarding Crowding Phenomena." *American Psychologist* 39, no. 10: 1148.

Creswell, John W., and Cheryl N. Poth. 2016. *Qualitative Inquiry and Research Design: Choosing Among Five Approaches*. Los Angeles: Sage Publications, Inc.

Crewe, Ben. 2005. "Prisoner Society in the Era of Hard Drugs." *Punishment & Society* 7, no. 4: 457–81.

Crewe, Ben. 2006. "Prison Drug Dealing and the Ethnographic Lens." *Howard Journal of Criminal Justice* 45, no. 4: 347–68.

Dalley, Lanette P. 2002. "Policy Implications Relating to Inmate Mothers and Their Children: Will the Past Be Prologue?" *Prison Journal* 82, no. 2: 234–68.

DeFina, Robert H., and Lance Hannon. 2010. "The Impact of Adult Incarceration on Child Poverty: A County-Level Analysis, 1995–2007." *Prison Journal* 90, no. 4: 377–96.

DeLisi, Matt, Mark T. Berg, and Andy Hochstetler. 2004. "Gang Members, Career Criminals and Prison Violence: Further Specification of the Importation Model of Inmate Behavior." *Criminal Justice Studies* 17, no. 4: 369–83.

Denzin, Norman K., and Michael D. Giardina. 2008. *Qualitative Inquiry and the Politics of Evidence*. Walnut Creek, CA: Left Coast Press.

Devlin, Angela. 1998. *"Invisible Women: What's Wrong with Women's Prisons?"*. Hampshire, UK: Waterside Press.

Dey, Ian. 2003. *Qualitative Data Analysis: A User Friendly Guide for Social Scientists*. London: Routledge.

Doyle, James A., and Michele Antoinette Paludi. 1991. *Sex and Gender: The Human Experience*. Dubuque, IA: Wm. C. Brown Company.

References   135

Drury, Alan J., and Matt DeLisi. 2011. "Gangkill: An Exploratory Empirical Assessment of Gang Membership, Homicide Offending, and Prison Misconduct." *Crime & Delinquency* 57, no. 1: 130–46.

Du Bois, William Edward Burghardt, 1903. *The Souls of Black Folk: Essays and Drawings*. Chicago: A. C. McClurg & Co.

Dufault-Hunter, Erin. 2012. *The Transformative Power of Faith: A Narrative Approach to Conversion*. Lanham, MD: Lexington Books.

Eddy, J. Mark, and John B. Reid. 2002. "The Antisocial Behavior of the Adolescent Children of Incarcerated Parents: A Developmental Perspective." In *Papers Prepared for the "From Prison to Home" Conference*. Washington, DC: The Urban Institute.

Edgar, Kimmett, and Ian O'Donnell. 1998. *Mandatory Drug Testing in Prisons: An Evaluation*. London: Home Office Research, Development and Statistics Directorate.

Eigenberg, Helen M. 1992. "Homosexuality in Male Prisons: Demonstrating the Need for a Social Constructionist Approach." *Criminal Justice Review* 17, no. 2: 219–34.

Einat, Tomer, and Haim Einat. 2000. "Inmate Argot as an Expression of Prison Subculture: The Israeli Case." *Prison Journal* 80, no. 3: 309–25.

Ettorre, Elizabeth M. 1992. *Women and Substance Use*. New Brunswick, NJ: Rutgers Univ. Press.

European Monitoring Centre for Drugs and Drug Addiction (EMCDDA). 2012. *Prisons and Drugs in Europe: The Problem and Responses*. Lisbon: European Monitoring Centre for Drugs and Drug Addiction (EMCDDA).

Evans, Tony, and Patti Wallace. 2008. "A Prison Within a Prison? The Masculinity Narratives of Male Prisoners." *Men and Masculinities* 10, no. 4: 484–507.

Farhadi, Asghar. Director. 2004. "Beautiful City," https://www.imdb.com/title/tt0424434/.

Farrington, David P., and Christopher P. Nuttall. 1980. "Prison Size, Overcrowding, Prison Violence, and Recidivism." *Journal of Criminal Justice* 8, no. 4: 221–31.

Flyvbjerg, Bent. 2006. "Five Misunderstandings About Case-Study Research." *Qualitative Inquiry* 12, no. 2: 219–45.

Fong, Robert S. 1990. "The Organizational Structure of Prison Gangs: A Texas Case Study." *Federal Probation* 54, no. 1: 36.

Fong, Robert S., and Salvador Buentello. 1991. "The Detection of Prison Gang Development: An Empirical Assessment." *Federal Probation* 55, no. 1: 66.

136   References

Fong, Robert S., Ronald E. Vogel, and Salvador Buentello. 1992. "Prison Gang Dynamics: A Look Inside the Texas Department of Corrections." In *Corrections: Dilemmas and Directions*, edited by Peter J. Benekos and Alida V. Merlo, 57–77. Ithaca, NY: Cornell Univ. Press.

Forsyth, Craig J., Rhonda D. Evans, and D. Burk Foster. 2002. "An Analysis of Inmate Explanations for Lesbian Relationships in Prison." *International Journal of Sociology of the Family* 30, no. 1/2, Spring and Autumn 2002: 67–77.

Foucault, Michel. 1973. *The Birth of the Clinic*. New York: Pantheon Books.

Foucault, Michel. 1979. *Discipline and Punish: The Birth of the Prison*. Translated by Alan Sheridan. New York: Vintage Books.

Foucault, Michel. 1980. *The History of Sexuality. Volume One: An Introduction*. New York: Vintage Books.

Foucault, Michel. 2007. *Security, Territory, Population: Lectures at the Collège de France, 1977–1978*. Translated by G. Burchell. New York: Palgrave Macmillan.

Friestad, Christine, and Inger Lise Skog Hansen. 2005. "Mental Health Problems Among Prison Inmates: The Effect of Welfare Deficiencies, Drug Use and Self-Efficacy." *Journal of Scandinavian Studies in Criminology and Crime Prevention* 6, no. 2: 183–96.

Fritsch, Travis A., and John D. Burkhead. 1981. "Behavioral Reactions of Children to Parental Absence Due to Imprisonment." *Family Relations* 30, no. 1: 83–88.

Gaes, Gerald G., and William J. McGuire. 1985. "Prison Violence: The Contribution of Crowding Versus Other Determinants of Prison Assault Rates." *Journal of Research in Crime and Delinquency* 22, no. 1: 41–65.

Gaes, Gerald G., Susan Wallace, Evan Gilman, Jody Klein-Saffran, and Sharon Suppa. 2002. "The Influence of Prison Gang Affiliation on Violence and Other Prison Misconduct." *Prison Journal* 82, no. 3: 359–85.

Galanter, Marc, Helen Dermatis, Stephen Post, and Cristal Sampson. 2013. "Spirituality-based Recovery from Drug Addiction in the Twelve-Step Fellowship of Narcotics Anonymous." *Journal of Addiction Medicine* 7, no. 3: 189–95.

Gasson, Susan. 2004. "Rigor in Grounded Theory Research: An Interpretive Perspective on Generating Theory from Qualitative Field Studies." In *The Handbook of Information Systems Research*, edited by Michael E. Whitman and Amy B. Woszczynski, 79–102. Hershey, PA: IGI Global.

Gear, Sasha. 2007. "Behind the Bars of Masculinity: Male Rape and Homophobia in and about South African Men's Prisons." *Sexualities* 10, no. 2: 209–27.

Gentles, Stephen J., Susan M. Jack, David B. Nicholas, and K. McKibbon. 2014. "A Critical Approach to Reflexivity in Grounded Theory." *Qualitative Report* 19, no. 44.

Ghiabi, Maziyar. 2015. "Drugs and Revolution in Iran: Islamic Devotion, Revolutionary Zeal and Republican Means." *Iranian Studies* 48, no. 2: 139–63.

Ghiabi, Maziyar. 2018. "Maintaining Disorder: The Micropolitics of Drugs Policy in Iran." *Third World Quarterly* 39, no. 2: 277–97.

Ghiabi, Maziyar. 2019. *Drugs Politics: Managing Disorder in the Islamic Republic of Iran*. Cambridge: Cambridge Univ. Press.

Giallombardo, Rose. 1966. "Social Roles in a Prison for Women." *Social Problems* 13, no. 3: 268–88.

Giallombardo, Rose. 1966. *Society of Women: A Study of a Women's Prison*. New York: Wiley.

Giddens, Anthony. 1990. *The Consequences of Modernity*. Stanford, CA: Stanford Univ. Press.

Giddens, A., and C. Pierson. 1998. *Conversations with Anthony Giddens: Making Sense of Modernity*. Stanford, CA: Stanford Univ. Press.

Gillespie, Wayne. 2002. *Prisonization: Individual and Institutional Factors Affecting Inmate Conduct*. New York: LFB Scholarly Publishing LLC.

Gillespie, Wayne. 2005. "A Multilevel Model of Drug Abuse Inside Prison." *Prison Journal* 85, no. 2: 223–46.

Giroux, Henry A. 1991. "Border Pedagogy and the Politics of Postmodernism." *Social Text* 28: 51–67.

Glaser, B. G., and A. L. Strauss. 1967. "The Discovery of Grounded Theory: Strategies for Qualitative Research; Aldine Transaction: New Brunswick, NJ, USA." In Library of Congress Catalog, no. 66–28314.

Glaser, Barney G. 1978. *Advances in the Methodology of Grounded Theory: Theoretical Sensitivity*. Mill Valley, CA: Sociology Press.

Glaser, Barney G. 1992. *Basics of Grounded Theory Analysis: Emergence vs. Forcing*. Mill Valley, CA: Sociology Press.

Glaser, Barney G., and Anselm L. Strauss. 2017. *Discovery of Grounded Theory: Strategies for Qualitative Research*. London: Routledge.

Goffman, Erving. 1962. *Asylums: Essays on the Social Situation of Mental Patients and Other Inmates*. Chicago: Aldine Transaction.

Golafshani, Nahid. 2003. "Understanding Reliability and Validity in Qualitative Research." *Qualitative Report* 8, no. 4: 597–607.

138   References

Graneheim, Ulla H., and Berit Lundman. 2004. "Qualitative Content Analysis in Nursing Research: Concepts, Procedures and Measures to Achieve Trustworthiness." *Nurse Education Today* 24, no. 2: 105–12.

Griffin, Marie L., and John R. Hepburn. 2006. "The Effect of Gang Affiliation on Violent Misconduct Among Inmates During the Early Years of Confinement." *Criminal Justice and Behavior* 33, no. 4: 419–66.

Grusky, Oscar. 1959. "Organizational Goals and the Behavior of Informal Leaders." *American Journal of Sociology* 65, no. 1: 59–67.

Guba, Egon G. 1990. *The Paradigm Dialog.* Thousand Oaks, CA: Sage Publications, Inc.

Gueta, Keren, Sharon Gamliel, and Natti Ronel. 2021. "'Weak Is the New Strong': Gendered Meanings of Recovery from Substance Abuse Among Male Prisoners Participating in Narcotic Anonymous Meetings." *Men and Masculinities* 24, no. 1: 104–26.

Hagan, John, and Ronit Dinovitzer. 1999. "Collateral Consequences of Imprisonment for Children, Communities, and Prisoners." *Crime and Justice* 26: 121–62.

Haj, Hosseini Mansooreh, and Ramin Hashemi. 2015. "Addicts' Quality of Life and Psychological Disorders (Depression, Anxiety, and Stress) in Two Treatment Methods: Narcotics Anonymous Vs. Methadone Maintenance Treatment." *Research on Addiction* 9, no. 35, 119–36.

Hall, Wendy A., and Peter Callery. 2001. "Enhancing the Rigor of Grounded Theory: Incorporating Reflexivity and Relationality." *Qualitative Health Research* 11, no. 2: 257–72.

Hampton, Blanche. 1994. *Prisons and Women.* Randwick, Australia: The Center for Professional Development Corrective Services, Univ. of New South Wales.

Hensley, Christopher Lee. 1995. "Social Reactance Towards Homosexuality: An Analysis of College Student's Attitudes." PhD diss., Mississippi State Univ.

Hensley, Christopher. 2000. "Attitudes Toward Homosexuality in a Male and Female Prison: An Exploratory Study." *Prison Journal* 80, no. 4: 434–41.

Herek, Gregory M. 1988. "Heterosexuals' Attitudes Toward Lesbians and Gay Men: Correlates and Gender Differences." *Journal of Sex Research* 25, no. 4: 451–77.

Herek, Gregory M., and John P. Capitanio. 1999. "Sex Differences in How Heterosexuals Think About Lesbians and Gay Men: Evidence from Survey Context Effects." *Journal of Sex Research* 36, no. 4: 348–60.

Hesse-Biber, Sharlene Nagy. 2010. *Mixed Methods Research: Merging Theory with Practice*. New York: Guilford Press.

Hissel, Sanne, Catrien Bijleveld, and Candace Kruttschnitt. 2011. "The Well-Being of Children of Incarcerated Mothers: An Exploratory Study for the Netherlands." *European Journal of Criminology* 8, no. 5: 346–60.

Howe, Adrian. 2005. *Punish and Critique: Towards a Feminist Analysis of Penality*. London: Routledge.

Hucklesby, Anthea, and Christine Wilkinson. 2001. "Drug Misuse in Prisons: Some Comments on the Prison Service Drug Strategy." *Howard Journal of Criminal Justice* 40, no. 4: 347–63.

Huebner, Beth M. 2003. "Administrative Determinants of Inmate Violence: A Multilevel Analysis." *Journal of Criminal Justice* 31, no. 2: 107–17.

Huff, C. Ronald, and Matthew Meyer. 1997. "Managing Prison Gangs and Other Security Threat Groups." *Corrections Management Quarterly* 1, no. 4: 10–18.

Hungerford, Gregory Patrick. 1993. "The Children of Inmate Mothers: An Exploratory Study of Children, Caretakers and Inmate Mothers in Ohio." PhD diss., Ohio State Univ.

Hunt, Geoffrey, Stephanie Riegel, Tomas Morales, and Dan Waldorf. 1993. "Changes in Prison Culture: Prison Gangs and the Case of the 'Pepsi Generation.'" *Social Problems* 40, no. 3: 398–409.

Hunter, Shireen T. 2014. "Can Hassan Rouhani Succeed Where Muhammad Khatami Failed? Internal and International Politics of Reform in Iran." *Contemporary Review of the Middle East* 1, no. 3: 253–68.

Hutter, Bridget, and Gillian Williams, eds. 1981. *Controlling Women: The Normal and the Deviant*. Vol. 4. London: Taylor & Francis.

Illich, Ivan. 1976. *Limits to Medicine, Medical Nemesis: The Expropriation of Health*. London: Penguin Books.

Iran Human Rights (IHR). 2016. *The Annual Report on the Death Penalty in Iran*.

Irwin, John, and Donald R. Cressey. 1962. "Thieves, Convicts and the Inmate Culture." *Social Problems* 10, no. 2: 142–55.

Javdani, Shabnam, Naomi Sadeh, and Edelyn Verona. 2011. "Expanding Our Lens: Female Pathways to Antisocial Behavior in Adolescence and Adulthood." *Clinical Psychology Review* 31, no. 8: 1324–48.

Jewkes, Yvonne. 2005. "Men Behind Bars: 'Doing' Masculinity as an Adaptation to Imprisonment." *Men and Masculinities* 8, no. 1: 44–63.

140 References

Jiang, Shanhe, and Marianne Fisher-Giorlando. 2002. "Inmate Misconduct: A Test of the Deprivation, Importation, and Situational Models." *Prison Journal* 82, no. 3: 335–58.

Johnson, Elizabeth I., and Jane Waldfogel. 2002. "Parental Incarceration: Recent Trends and Implications for Child Welfare." *Social Service Review* 76, no. 3: 460–79.

Johnson, Rucker. 2009. "Ever-Increasing Levels of Parental Incarceration and the Consequences for Children." In *Do Prisons Make Us Safer: The Benefits and Costs of the Prison Boom*, edited by Steven Raphael and Michael A. Stoll, 177–206. New York: Russell Sage Foundation.

Kamiński, Marek M., and Don C. Gibbons. 1994. "Prison Subculture in Poland." *Crime & Delinquency* 40, no. 1: 105–19.

Karimi, Neda, and Sepideh Gharaati. 2013. "Why Do Brains Drain? Brain Drain in Iran's Political Discourse." *Cadaad Journal* 6, no. 2: 154–73.

Kaskutas, Lee Ann. 2009. "Alcoholics Anonymous Effectiveness: Faith Meets Science." *Journal of Addictive Diseases* 28, no. 2: 145–57.

Kellner, Douglas. 1992. "Popular Culture and the Construction of Postmodern Identities." In *Modernity and Identity*, edited by L. Friedman, 141–77. Oxford: Blackwell.

Kelly, John F., and Julie D. Yeterian. 2008. "Mutual-Help Groups for Dually Diagnosed Individuals: Rationale, Description, and Review of the Evidence." *Journal of Groups in Addiction & Recovery* 3, no. 3–4: 217–42.

Kelly, Liz, and Jill Radford. 1987. "The Problem of Men: Feminist Perspectives on Sexual Violence." *Law, Order and the Authoritarian State*: 237–79.

Khoshnood, K., F. Hashemian, N. Moshtagh, M. Eftekahri, and S. Setayesh. 2008. "T03-O-08 Social Stigma, Homosexuality and Transsexuality in Iran." *Sexologies* 17: S69.

Khosravi, Shahram. 2008. *Young and Defiant in Tehran*. Philadelphia: Univ. of Pennsylvania Press.

Kianpour, Masoud. 2016. "From Heaven to Earth: Interpretations and Conceptualizations of Human Dignity in Iran." *Comparative Sociology* 15, no. 6: 699–723.

Kite, Mary E., and Bernard E. Whitley Jr. 1996. "Sex Differences in Attitudes Toward Homosexual Persons, Behaviors, and Civil Rights: A Meta-Analysis." *Personality and Social Psychology Bulletin* 22, no. 4: 336–53.

Kohn, Marek. 1992. *Dope Girls: The Birth of the British Drug Underground*. London: Granta Books.

Koscheski, Mary, and Christopher Hensley. 2001. "Inmate Homosexual Behavior in a Southern Female Correctional Facility." *American Journal of Criminal Justice* 25, no. 2: 269–77.

Kurdek, Lawrence A. 1988. "Perceived Social Support in Gays and Lesbians in Cohabitating Relationships." *Journal of Personality and Social Psychology* 54, no. 3: 504.

LaMar, Lisa, and Mary Kite. 1998. "Sex Differences in Attitudes Toward Gay Men and Lesbians: A Multidimensional Perspective." *Journal of Sex Research* 35, no. 2: 189–96.

Laub, John H., and Robert J. Sampson. 2001. "Understanding Desistance from Crime." *Crime and Justice* 28: 1–69.

Lawrence, Claire, and Kathryn Andrews. 2004. "The Influence of Perceived Prison Crowding on Male Inmates' Perception of Aggressive Events." *Aggressive Behavior*: 30, no. 4: 273–83.

Leger, Robert G. 1987. "Lesbianism among Women Prisoners: Participants and Nonparticipants." *Criminal Justice and Behavior* 14, no. 4: 448–67.

Lidz, Charles W., and Andrew L. Walker. 1980. *Heroin, Deviance and Morality*. Beverly Hills, CA: Sage Publications, Inc.

Liebling, Alison, and Helen Arnold. 2004. *Prisons and Their Moral Performance: A Study of Values, Quality, and Prison Life*. Oxford: Oxford Univ. Press.

Lincoln, Y., and E. Guba. 1985. *Naturalistic Inquiry*. Vol. 75. Beverly Hills: Sage Publications, Inc.

Lockwood, Daniel. 1980. *Prison Sexual Violence*. New York: Elsevier.

Lune, Howard, and Bruce L. Berg. 2017. *Qualitative Research Methods for the Social Sciences*. Boston: Pearson.

Maccoby, Eleanor E. 1987. "The Varied Meanings of 'Masculine' and 'Feminine.'" In *Masculinity/Femininity: Basic Perspectives*, edited by June Machover Reinisch, Leonard A. Rosenblum, and Stephanie A. Sanders, 227–39. New York: Oxford Univ. Press.

Mackenzie, Noella, and Sally Knipe. 2006. "Research Dilemmas: Paradigms, Methods and Methodology." *Issues in Educational Research* 16, no. 2: 193–205.

Madani Qahrfarkhi, Saeed. 2011. *E'tiyad Dar Iran*. Tehran: Nashr-e Sales.

Maghsoudi, A., Anaraki, N. R., and Boostani, D. 2018. "Patriarchy as a Contextual and Gendered Pathway to Crime: A Qualitative Study of Iranian Women Offenders." *Quality & Quantity* 52, no. 1, 355–70.

Mahdavi, Pardis. 2007. "Passionate Uprisings: Young People, Sexuality and Politics in Post-Revolutionary Iran." *Culture, Health & Sexuality* 9, no. 5: 445–57.

142   References

Mahmoudi, Hassan. 2021, April 22. "Iran Loses Highly Educated and Skilled Citizens during Long-Running "Brain Drain." *Migration Information Source*. https://www.migrationpolicy.org/article/iran-brain-drain-emigration.

Mahoney, Michael J. 1980. "Psychotherapy and the Structure of Personal Revolutions." In *Psychotherapy Process: Current Issues and Future Directions*, edited by Michael J. Mahoney, 157–80. Boston, MA: Springer.

Malloch, Margaret. 2001. *Women, Drugs and Custody: The Experiences of Women Drug Users in Prison*. Winchester, UK: Waterside Press.

Malloch, Margaret. 2011. "Interventions for Drug Users in the Criminal Justice System: Scottish Review." Research Report No. 05/2011. www.sccjr.ac.uk.

Maltz, Michael D. 1984. *Recidivism*. Orlando, FL: Academic Press.

Manuel, Tiffany. 2007. "Envisioning the Possibilities for a Good Life: Exploring the Public Policy Implications of Intersectionality Theory." *Journal of Women, Politics & Policy* 28, no. 3–4: 173–203.

Martinson, Robert. 1974. "What works?—Questions and Answers About Prison Reform." *Public Interest* 35: 22.

Matthee, Rudi. 2005. *The Pursuit of Pleasure: Drugs and Stimulants in Iranian History, 1500–1900*. Princeton: Princeton Univ. Press.

McCoy, Lisa K., John A. Hermos, Barbara G. Bokhourm, and Susan M. Frayne. 2005. "Conceptual Bases of Christian, Faith-Based Substance Abuse Rehabilitation Programs: Qualitative Analysis of Staff Interviews." *Substance Abuse* 25, no. 3: 1–11.

McDonald, Kevin. 1994. "Alain Touraine's Sociology of the Subject." *Thesis Eleven* 38, no. 1: 46–60.

Megargee, Edwin I. 1976. "Population Density and Disruptive Behavior in a Prison Setting." *Prison Violence*: 135–44.

Minichiello, Victor, Rosalie Aroni, and Terrence Neville Hays. 2008. *In-Depth Interviewing: Principles, Techniques, Analysis*. Frenchs Forest, Australia: Pearson Education Australia.

Mjåland, Kristian. 2014. "'A Culture of Sharing': Drug Exchange in a Norwegian Prison." *Punishment & Society* 16, no. 3: 336–52.

Mjåland, Kristian. 2016. "Exploring Prison Drug Use in the Context of Prison-Based Drug Rehabilitation." *Drugs: Education, Prevention, and Policy* 23, no. 2: 154–62.

Mokri, Azarakhsh. 2002. "Brief Overview of the Status of Drug Abuse in Iran." *Archives of Iranian Medicine* 5, no. 3: 184–90.

Molavi, Afshin. 2010. *The Soul of Iran: A Nation's Struggle for Freedom*. New York: W. W. Norton and Company.

Moradi, Ghobad, Marzieh Farnia, Mostafa Shokoohi, Mohammad Shahbazi, Babak Moazen, and Khaled Rahmani. 2015. "Methadone Maintenance Treatment Program in Prisons from the Perspective of Medical and Non-Medical Prison Staff: A Qualitative Study in Iran." *International Journal of Health Policy and Management* 4, no. 9: 583.

Morrissey, Elizabeth R. 1986. "Power and Control Through Discourse: The Case of Drinking and Drinking Problems Among Women." *Crime, Law and Social Change* 10, no. 2: 157.

Morse, Janice M., Michael Barrett, Maria Mayan, Karin Olson, and Jude Spiers. 2002. "Verification Strategies for Establishing Reliability and Validity in Qualitative Research." *International Journal of Qualitative Methods* 1, no. 2: 13–22.

Murray, Joseph, David P. Farrington, Ivana Sekol, and Rikke F. Olsen. 2009. "Effects of Parental Imprisonment on Child Antisocial Behaviour and Mental Health: A Systematic Review." *Campbell Systematic Reviews* 5, no. 1: 1–105.

Nacci, Peter L., and Thomas R. Kane. 1984. "Sex and Sexual Aggression in Federal Prisons." *Federal Probation* 48: 46.

Narcotics Anonymous World Services, Inc. 1993. *It Works: How and Why: The Twelve Steps and Twelve Traditions of Narcotics Anonymous*. Chatsworth, CA: Narcotics Anonymous World Services, Inc.

Narcotics Anonymous World Services, Inc. 2006. *Public Relations Handbook*. Chatsworth, CA: Narcotics Anonymous World Services, Inc.

Narcotics Anonymous World Services, Inc. 2021. *Annual Report*. Chatsworth, CA: Narcotics Anonymous World Services, Inc.

Neff, James Alan, and Samuel A. MacMaster. 2005. "Applying Behavior Change Models to Understand Spiritual Mechanisms Underlying Change in Substance Abuse Treatment." *American Journal of Drug and Alcohol Abuse* 31, no. 4: 669–84.

Newton, Carolyn. 1994. "Gender Theory and Prison Sociology: Using Theories of Masculinities to Interpret the Sociology of Prisons for Men." *Howard Journal of Criminal Justice* 33, no. 3: 193–202.

Nikpour, Golnar. 2018. *Drugs and Drug Policy in the Islamic Republic of Iran*. Waltham, MA: Brandeis Univ. Crown Center for Middle East Studies.

144   References

Nissaramanesh, Bijan, Mike Trace, and Marcus Roberts. 2005. "The Rise of Harm Reduction in the Islamic Republic of Iran." Beckley Foundation Drug Policy Programme, Briefing Paper 8.

Noaks, Lesley, and Emma Wincup. 2004. "Using Documentary Evidence in Qualitative Research." *Criminological Research*. London: Sage Publications, Inc., 106–20.

Ohiri, Kelechi, Mariam Claeson, E. Rassaghi, B. Nassirimanesh, P. Afshar, and R. Power. 2006. "HIV/AIDS Prevention Among Injection Drug Users: Learning from Harm Reduction in Iran." Iran: HIV Prevention Consultation: 17–20.

Ohlin, Lloyd E. 1956. "Sociology and the Field of Corrections." Russell Sage Foundation *Criminal Area Pamphlets* 13, no. 6.

Oleinik, Anton. 2013. "The Social Life of Illegal Drug Users in Prison: A Comparative Perspective." *European Journal of Crime, Criminal Law and Criminal Justice* 21, no. 2: 185–206.

Oleinik, Anton. 2016. "Honor and Human Rights: A Comparative Study of Russia and Ukraine." *Comparative Sociology* 15, no. 6: 669–98.

Oleinik, Anton N. 2017. *Organized Crime, Prison, and Post-Soviet Societies*. London: Routledge.

Owen, Barbara. 1998. *In the Mix: Struggle and Survival in a Women's Prison*. Albany, NY: State Univ. of New York Press.

Pelissier, Bernadette. 1991. "The Effects of a Rapid Increase in a Prison Population: A Pre- and Posttest Study." *Criminal Justice and Behavior* 18, no. 4: 427–47.

Pervin, M. (2016). "Law of Murder Under Islamic Criminal Law: An Analysis." *Journal of Law, Policy and Globalization* 53, 143.

Peyrot, Mark. 1985. "Narcotics Anonymous: Its History, Structure, and Approach." *International Journal of the Addictions* 20, no. 10: 1509–22.

Pitch, Tamar. 1995. *Limited Responsibilities: Social Movements and Criminal Justice*. London: Routledge.

Plugge, Emma, Patricia Yudkin, and Nicola Douglas. 2009. "Changes in Women's Use of Illicit Drugs Following Imprisonment." *Addiction* 104, no. 2: 215–22.

Plugge-Foust, Carol, and George Strickland. 2000. "Homophobia, Irrationality, and Christian Ideology: Does a Relationship Exist?" *Journal of Sex Education and Therapy* 25, no. 4: 240–44.

Poehlmann, Julie. 2005. "Children's Family Environments and Intellectual Outcomes During Maternal Incarceration." *Journal of Marriage and Family* 67, no. 5: 1275–85.

References   145

Pollock, Joycelyn M. 1998. *Counseling Women in Prison*. Thousand Oaks, CA: Sage Publications, Inc.

Ponterotto, Joseph G. and Ingrid Grieger. 1999. "Merging Qualitative and Quantitative Perspectives in a Research Identity." In *Using Qualitative Methods in Psychology*, edited by M. Kopala and L. A. Suzuki, 49–62. Thousand Oaks, CA: Sage Publication, Inc.

Price, Jammie, and Michael G. Dalecki. 1998. "The Social Basis of Homophobia: An Empirical Illustration." *Sociological Spectrum* 18, no. 2: 143–59.

Propper, Alice M. 1982. "Make-Believe Families and Homosexuality Among Imprisoned Girls." *Criminology* 20, no. 1: 127–38.

Radio Farda. July 15, 2019. *Iranian Use More Than Two Tons of Narcotics Every Day*. https://en.radiofarda.com/a/iranian-use-more-than-two-tons-of-narcotics -every-day/30056090.html.

Ralph, P. H., and J. W. Marquart. 1991. "Gang Violence in Texas Prisons." *Prison Journal* 71, no. 2: 38–49.

Razzaghi, E., Afarin Rahimi, M. Hosseini, and A. Chatterjee. 1999. *Rapid Situation Assessment (RSA) of Drug Abuse in Iran*. Prevention Department, State Welfare Organization, Ministry of Health, IR of Iran and United Nations International Drug Control Program.

Reisig, Michael D. 2002. "Administrative Control and Inmate Homicide." *Homicide Studies* 6, no. 1: 84–103.

Reuters, August 27, 2016. "Death Penalty Failing to Deter Drug Trafficking in Iran: Official." https://www.reuters.com/article/us-iran-rights-executions /death-penalty-failing-to-deter-drug-trafficking-in-iran-official-idUSKCN 1120A8.

Richmond, Katy. 1978. "Fear of Homosexuality and Modes of Rationalisation in Male Prisons." *Australian and New Zealand Journal of Sociology* 14, no. 1: 51–57.

Robinson, Jennifer, Jitender Sareen, Brian J. Cox, and James Bolton. 2009. "Self-Medication of Anxiety Disorders with Alcohol and Drugs: Results from a Nationally Representative Sample." *Journal of Anxiety Disorders* 23, no. 1: 38–45.

Roustayi, Saeed. Director. 2004. "Life and a Day." https://www.imdb.com/title /tt5460658/.

Ruback, R. Barry, and Timothy S. Carr. 1993. "Prison Crowding Over Time: The Relationship of Density and Changes in Density to Infraction Rates." *Criminal Justice and Behavior* 20, no. 2: 130–48.

146   References

Rymhs, Deena. 2012. "In This Inverted Garden: Masculinities in Canadian Prison Writing." *Journal of Gender Studies* 21, no. 1: 77–89.

Sagarin, Edward. 1976. "Prison Homosexuality and Its Effect on Post-Prison Sexual Behavior." *Psychiatry* 39, no. 3: 245–57.

Sampson, Robert J., and Janet L. Lauritsen. 1994. "Violent Victimization and Offending: Individual, Situational, and Community-Level Factors." In *Understanding and Preventing Violence: Social Influences, Vol. 3*, edited by Albert J. Reiss Jr. and Jeffrey A. Roth, 1–114. Washington, DC: National Academy Press.

Sanders, Jolene. 2014. *Women in Narcotics Anonymous: Overcoming Stigma and Shame*. London: Palgrave Macmillan.

Saum, Christine A., Hilary L. Surratt, James A. Inciardi, and Rachael E. Bennett. 1995. "Sex in Prison: Exploring the Myths and Realities." *Prison Journal* 75, no. 4: 413–30.

Schwartz, Barry. 1971. "Pre-Institutional vs. Situational Influence in a Correctional Community." *Journal of Criminal Law, Criminology, and Police Science* 62, no. 4: 532–42.

Seltzer, Richard. 1992. "The Social Location of Those Holding Antihomosexual Attitudes." *Sex Roles* 26, no. 9–10: 391–98.

Sheeran, Scott, and Nigel S. Rodley, eds. 2013. *Routledge Handbook of International Human Rights Law*. London: Routledge.

Shelden, Randall G. 1991. "A Comparison of Gang Members and Non-Gang Members in a Prison Setting." *Prison Journal* 71, no. 2: 50–60.

Siamdoust, Nahid. 2017. *Soundtrack of the Revolution: The Politics of Music in Iran*. Stanford, CA: Stanford Univ. Press.

Sigelman, Carol K., Jennifer L. Howell, David P. Cornell, John D. Cutright, and Janine C. Dewey. 1991. "Courtesy Stigma: The Social Implications of Associating with a Gay Person." *Journal of Social Psychology* 131, no. 1: 45–56.

Singer, Linda. 1992. *Erotic Welfare: Sexual Theory and Politics in the Age of Epidemic*. London: Routledge.

Sirisutthidacha, Warissara, and Dittita Tititampruk. 2014. "Patterns of Inmate Subculture: A Qualitative Study of Thai Inmates." *International Journal of Criminal Justice Sciences* 9, no. 1: 94.

Slosar, John A. 1978. *Prisonization, Friendship, and Leadership*. Lexington, MA: Lexington Books.

Smart, Carol, and Julia Brophy, eds. 1985. *Women-In-Law: Explorations in Law, Family, and Sexuality*. London: Routledge and Kegan Paul.

Smith, Mary Lee. 1987. "Publishing Qualitative Research." *American Educational Research Journal* 24, no. 2: 173–83.

Smith, Peter Scharff, and Lucy Gampell, eds. 2011. *Children of Imprisoned Parents*. Copenhagen: Danish Institute for Human Rights.

Snacken, Sonja. 2006. "A Reductionist Penal Policy and European Human Rights Standards." *European Journal on Criminal Policy and Research* 12, no. 2: 143–64.

Snyder, L. 2002. "Confidentiality and Anonymity: Promises and Practices." In *Walking the Tightrope: Ethical Issues for Qualitative Researchers*, edited by W. C. van den Hoonaard, 70–78. Toronto: Univ. of Toronto Press.

Sparks, Richard, Anthony Bottoms, and Will Hay. 1996. *Prisons and the Problem of Order*. Oxford: Oxford Univ. Press.

Stevens, Dennis J. 1997. "Origins and Effects of Prison Drug Gangs in North Carolina." *Journal of Gang Research* 4, no. 4: 23–35.

Stevens, Dennis J. 1997. "Prison Regime and Drugs." *Howard Journal of Criminal Justice* 36, no. 1: 14–27.

Stover, H., and C. Weilandt. 2007. "Drug Use and Drug Services in Prison. In *Health in Prisons: A WHO Guide to the Essentials in Prison Health*, 85–111. Copenhagen: WHO Regional Office for Europe.

Strang, John, Michael Gossop, Joan Heuston, John Green, Christopher Whiteley, and Anthony Maden. 2006. "Persistence of Drug Use During Imprisonment: Relationship of Drug Type, Recency of Use and Severity of Dependence to Use of Heroin, Cocaine and Amphetamine in Prison." *Addiction* 101, no. 8: 1125–32.

Struckman-Johnson, Cindy, David Struckman-Johnson, Lila Rucker, Kurt Bumby, and Stephen Donaldson. 1996. "Sexual Coercion Reported by Men and Women in Prison." *Journal of Sex Research* 33, no. 1: 67–76.

Sykes, G. M. 1958. *The Society of Captives: A Study of a Maximum Security Prison*. Princeton: Princeton Univ. Press.

Sykes, Gresham M. 2021. *The Society of Captives*. Princeton: Princeton Univ. Press.

Taylor, Avril. 1993. *Women Drug Users: An Ethnography of a Female Injecting Community*. Oxford: Oxford Univ. Press.

Tewksbury, Richard. 1989. "Fear of Sexual Assault in Prison Inmates." *Prison Journal* 69, no. 1: 62–71.

Tewksbury, Richard. 2013. "Qualitative Versus Quantitative Methods: Understanding Why Qualitative Methods Are Superior for Criminology and

148   References

Criminal Justice." In *The Handbook on Deviance*, edited by Erich Goode, 210–24. Chichester, England: Wiley Blackwell.

Thomas, Charles W. 1977. "Theoretical Perspectives on Prisonization: A Comparison of the Importation and Deprivation Models." *Journal of Criminal Law and Criminology* 68, no. 1: 135–45.

Thomas, Charles W., and Matthew T. Zingraff. 1976. "Organizational Structure as a Determinant of Prisonization: An Analysis of the Consequences of Alienation." *Pacific Sociological Review* 19, no. 1: 98–116.

Thomas, Charles W., and Samuel C. Foster. 1972. "Prisonization in the Inmate Contraculture." *Social Problems* 20, no. 2: 229–39.

Thompson, S. Anthony. 2016. "My Research Friend? My Friend the Researcher? My Friend, My Researcher? Mis/Informed Consent and People with Developmental Disabilities." In *Walking the Tightrope: Ethical Issues for Qualitative Researchers*, edited by W. C. van den Hoonaard, 95–106. Toronto: Univ. of Toronto Press.

Tittle, Charles R. 1969. "Inmate Organization: Sex Differentiation and the Influence of Criminal Subcultures." *American Sociological Review* 34, no. 6: 492–505.

Toch, Hans. 1998. "Hypermasculinity and Prison Violence." In *Masculinities and Violence*, edited by L. H. Bowker, 168–78. Thousand Oaks, CA: Sage Publication, Inc.

Toch, Hans, and Kenneth Adams. 1989. *The Disturbed Violent Offender*. New Haven: Yale Univ. Press.

Toch, Hans, and Terry A. Kupers. 2007. "Violence in Prisons, Revisited." *Journal of Offender Rehabilitation* 45, no. 3–4: 1–28.

Toch, Hans, Kenneth Adams, and J. Douglas Grant. 1989. *Coping: Maladaptation in Prisons*. Piscataway, NJ: Transaction Publishers.

Touraine, Alain. 1995. *Critique of Modernity*. Translated by D. Macey. Oxford: Basil Blackwell.

United Nation News, April 14, 2016, "Iran: UN Rights Chief Calls for End to Executions for Drug Offences."

United Nations Office on Drugs and Crime (UNODC), *World Drug Report*. 2012. Vienna: UNODC.

Useem, Bert. 1985. "Disorganization and the New Mexico Prison Riot of 1980." *American Sociological Review* 50, no.4: 677–88.

Van de Ven, Paul. 1994. "Comparisons among Homophobic Reactions of Undergraduates, High School Students, and Young Offenders." *Journal of Sex Research* 31, no. 2: 117–24.

Van den Hoonaard, Deborah Kestin. 2012. *Qualitative Research in Action: A Canadian Primer*. Don Mills, Ontario: Oxford Univ. Press Canada.

Varzi, Roxanne. 2006. *Warring Souls: Youth, Media, and Martyrdom in Post-Revolution Iran*. Durham, NC: Duke Univ. Press.

Vaughn, Michael S., and Allen D. Sapp. 1989. "Less Than Utopian: Sex Offender Treatment in a Milieu of Power Struggles, Status Positioning, and Inmate Manipulation in State Correctional Institutions." *Prison Journal* 69, no. 2: 73–89.

Wacquant, L. 2002. "The Curious Eclipse of Prison Ethnography in the Age of Mass Incarceration." *Ethnography* 3, no. 4, 371–97.

Ward, David A., and Gene G. Kassebaum. 1964. "Homosexuality: A Mode of Adaptation in a Prison for Women." *Social Problems* 12, No. 2: 159.

Weber, Max. 2017. *Methodology of Social Sciences*. London: Routledge.

Weinberg, Merlinda. 2016. "Biting the Hand That Feeds You, and Other Feminist Dilemmas in Fieldwork." In *Walking the Tightrope: Ethical Issues for Qualitative Researchers*, edited by W. C. van den Hoonaard, 79–94. Toronto: Univ. of Toronto Press.

Wellford, Charles. 1967. "Factors Associated with Adoption of the Inmate Code: A Study of Normative Socialization." *Journal of Criminal Law, Criminology, and Police Science* 58, no. 2: 197–203.

Wheeler, Stanton. 1961. "Socialization in Correctional Communities." *American Sociological Review* 26, no. 5: 697–712.

White, W. 2010. "The Future of AA, NA and Other Recovery Mutual Aid Organizations." *Counselor* 11, no. 2: 10–19.

Whittemore, Robin, Susan K. Chase, and Carol Lynn Mandle. 2001. "Validity in Qualitative Research." *Qualitative Health Research* 11, no. 4: 522–37.

Wieviorka, Michel. 2004. "The Making of Differences." *International Sociology* 19, no. 3: 281–97.

Williams, Kimberly M. *Learning Limits: College Women, Drugs, and Relationships*. 1998. London: Bergin and Garvey.

Willis, Katie, and Catherine Rushforth. 2003. "The Female Criminal: An Overview of Women's Drug Use and Offending Behaviour." *Trends and Issues in Crime and Criminal Justice* January 2003, no. 264.

Willis, Paul, and Mats Trondman. 2000. "Manifesto for Ethnography." *Ethnography* 1, no. 1: 5–16.

Windsor, Liliane Cambraia, and Clay Shorkey. 2010. "Spiritual Change in Drug Treatment: Utility of the Christian Inventory of Spirituality." *Substance Abuse* 31, no. 3: 136–45.

150 References

Winfree, L. Thomas Jr., Greg Newbold, and S. Houston Tubb III. 2002. "Prisoner Perspectives on Inmate Culture in New Mexico and New Zealand: A Descriptive Case Study." *Prison Journal* 82, no. 2: 213–33.

Witcher, Chad S. G. 2010. "Negotiating Transcription as a Relative Insider: Implications for Rigor." *International Journal of Qualitative Methods* 9, no. 2: 122–32.

Wood, Jane. 2006. "Gang Activity in English Prisons: The Prisoners' Perspective." *Psychology, Crime & Law* 12, no. 6: 605–17.

Wood, Jane, Alice Moir, and Mark James. 2009. "Prisoners' Gang-Related Activity: The Importance of Bullying and Moral Disengagement." *Psychology, Crime & Law* 15, no. 6: 569–81.

Wood, Jane, and Joanna Adler. 2001. "Gang Activity in English Prisons: The Staff Perspective." *Psychology, Crime & Law* 7, no. 2: 167–92.

Wood, Jane, Graham Ross Williams, and Mark James. 2010. "Incapacitation and Imprisonment: Prisoners' Involvement in Community-Based Crime." *Psychology, Crime & Law* 16, no. 7: 601–15.

Wooden, Wayne S. 2012. *Men behind Bars: Sexual Exploitation in Prison*. New York: Springer Science & Business Media.

Wooldredge, John, Timothy Griffin, and Travis Pratt. 2001. "Considering Hierarchical Models for Research on Inmate Behavior: Predicting Misconduct with Multilevel Data." *Justice Quarterly* 18, no. 1: 203–31.

Worrall, John L., and Robert G. Morris. 2012. "Prison Gang Integration and Inmate Violence." *Journal of Criminal Justice* 40, no. 5: 425–32.

Wortley, Richard. 2002. *Situational Prison Control: Crime Prevention in Correctional Institutions*. Cambridge: Cambridge Univ. Press.

Zahn, Margaret A. 2007. "The Causes of Girls' Delinquency and Their Program Implications." *Family Court Review* 45, no. 3: 456–65.

Zimmt, Raz. 2018. "The Effect of Economic and Social Processes on Iranian Foreign Policy." In *Iran in a Changing Strategic Environment, Memorandum No. 173*, edited by Meir Litvak, Emily B. Landau, and Ephraim Kam, 80. Tel-Aviv: The Institute for National Security Studies.

Zola, Irving Kenneth. 1983. "Culture and Symptoms: An Analysis of Patients' Presenting Complaints." In *Socio-Medical Inquiries, Recollections, Reflections, and Reconsiderations*, edited by Irving Kenneth Zola, 86–108.

Index

abstinence-based methods, 75
Afghanistan, 19, 21, 47, 50
Ahmadinejad, Mahmud, 24
anti-narcotic law, 14, 15, 19, 20, 25, 30, 54
Arak, 28

blood money, 63

capital punishment, 71
civil society, 6, 23
coercive approach, 2, 9, 92, 124
compulsory camps, 10, 15, 18, 20, 27,
    54–56, 111–12, 127
Constitutional Revolution, 18
contested identity, 15, 111–25
correctional officers, 48–51, 56, 58–59,
    64, 69–72, 115
crime-oriented approach, 21, 31, 42, 88,
    124, 126
criminalization, 2–5, 8, 27, 112–13,
    116–17, 123–26
critical case, 4, 11, 14–15

death penalty, 20, 26, 30–31, 63, 71
decriminalization, 24, 112
dehumanization, 37, 39, 41, 107
depression, 25, 57

detoxification, 18, 20, 23, 27, 40, 92, 114
drop-in centers, 10, 12–13, 15, 23, 91–92
drug business, 58, 61–62, 70, 112
drug-free lifestyle, 5, 33, 37, 57, 118, 121,
    125
drug smuggling, 45, 62–63
drug trafficker, 49–50
drug treatment camps, 5–9, 12, 13, 28, 75

economic crisis, 9, 30
empowerment, 106
equality, 78–79, 106
execution, 19, 22, 31, 71–72

Foucault, Michel, 3, 6, 8, 127

governmental organization, 1, 9–10, 29
Green Movement, 24, 30

harm reduction centers, 4, 7, 23–24,
    26–29, 116, 126–28
heroin injection, 8, 21, 22
higher power, 75, 97–98, 102
high-status criminals, 42, 48–49, 51, 62,
    69–72
HIV/AIDS, 22–23

152 Index

homosexual activities, 51–52
honor, 101–3, 106
humanitarian, 27, 123–25

identity, 43, 46, 65, 93–125
illegal camps, 28–29, 75, 92
illegal treatment centers, 1, 10, 28–29,
   75, 92
incarcerated women, 1, 45, 55, 114
informants, 41–42, 72–73
Iran Drug Control Headquarters, 6,
   21–22, 127
Iran-Iraq War, 19
Isfahan, 10, 28, 45, 103
Islamic Revolution, 19, 34
Islamic Revolutionary Guards, 20, 30

Karroubi, Mehdi, 24
Kerman, 10
Kermanshah, 23
Khatami, Mohammad, 22–24
Kurdistan, 39

law enforcement, 2–8, 21–23, 82, 123
long-term recovery, 2, 77, 79–81, 85–86,
   96–97

Mazandaran, 10, 18
medical-oriented approach, 4, 21, 89,
   112, 123, 126
methadone, 18–24, 52–54, 59
methadone maintenance treatment, 3, 8,
   23, 53, 66, 112
methamphetamine, 22, 25–26, 33, 43
Ministry of Health, 9, 12, 23–25, 27
Musavi, Mir Hossein, 24

Narcotics Anonymous, 1, 8, 74
NA subculture, 66–68, 107, 117, 119
nongovernmental organization, 1, 4, 10,
   26–27, 29, 91–92, 118, 124
normal, 3, 76, 93–95, 119–20, 122, 125
normalcy, 76, 88, 116

opium, 17–25
opium cultivation, 18, 21
ordinary citizens, 17, 29, 75, 81, 117, 125

patient, 2–3, 8, 15–16, 27, 93, 124–25, 128
patient criminal, 27
Persepolis NGO, 23
polyamorous, 99, 104–5, 110
poly-exclusion, 37
powerlessness, 15, 97, 103, 106, 113
prison gangs, 41, 42, 50
prison subculture, 15, 39, 56
privacy, 49, 115
private camps, 26–27, 29
privatization, 21
pseudo-medicalization, 116
psychological violence 30
punishment, 5–7, 21, 26–27, 31, 123, 126
punitive approach, 21–22, 27, 123, 126
purification plan, 56

Qajar reign, 17
quota system, 18

rehabilitation, 8–10, 59, 63, 66, 106, 124
reintegration, 88–89, 94, 103, 109, 117,
   119, 122
religion, 3, 5, 19, 37, 65, 75
Rouhani, Hasan, 30

Index   153

Safavid reign, 17

shame, 11, 51, 78, 82–83, 107, 114, 119

social capital, 46, 49, 68, 89

spiritual transformation, 66, 80–81, 97–98

sponsee, 80, 85, 126

sponsor, 74, 79–81, 85–86, 92–93, 97, 126

state-run camps, 1–2, 8–10, 12–13, 18, 20, 26–27, 29, 127

stigma, 7–8, 11, 27, 37, 51, 82–85, 101, 103

stigmatization, 27, 37, 83, 95, 101, 103–4, 108

surveillance, 2, 20, 23, 42, 64, 72, 107, 115

Tehran, 10, 23

transformation, 7, 66, 82, 93, 97–98, 119

transparency, 48–49, 84, 115

treatment-oriented approach, 3, 5, 113, 126

triangular clinics, 23

trust, 42, 70–73, 76, 82–116

twelve-step philosophy, 23, 27, 74

unemployment, 9, 20, 24, 30, 98

war on drugs, 20–21, 26, 29, 37, 94

welfare organizations, 6, 27

Nahid Rahimipour Anaraki is a postdoctoral fellow at Memorial University of Newfoundland and Labrador, Canada. She holds an MA in sociology from the University of Kerman, Iran, and a PhD in sociology from Memorial University. She is the author of *Prison in Iran: A Known Unknown* (Palgrave Macmillan, 2021) and several articles, both co- and single-authored, in the areas of sociology, criminology, and health sciences in *Quality & Quantity, Incarceration: An International Journal of Imprisonment, Implementation Science Communications Journal, Canadian Journal of Rural Medicine*, and *JMIR research protocols*.

Printed in the USA
CPSIA information can be obtained
at www.ICGtesting.com
LVHW032131090923
757492LV00023B/37